THE INVENTION OF THE MOVING ASSEMBLY LINE

A REVOLUTION IN MANUFACTURING

MILESTONES
IN AMERICAN HISTORY

THE INVENTION OF THE MOVING ASSEMBLY LINE

A REVOLUTION IN MANUFACTURING

DENNIS ABRAMS

CHELSEA HOUSE
An Infobase Learning Company

The Invention of the Moving Assembly Line

Copyright © 2011 by Infobase Learning

Chelsea House
An imprint of Infobase Learning
132 West 31st Street
New York, NY 10001

Library of Congress Cataloging-in-Publication Data

Abrams, Dennis, 1960–
The invention of the moving assembly line: a revolution in manufacturing/by Dennis Abrams.
    p.   cm. — (Milestones in American history)
Includes bibliographical references and index.
ISBN 978-1-60413-772-9 (hardcover)
1. Assembly-line methods—United States—History—Juvenile literature. I. Title.

TS178.4.A24 2011
670.42—dc22   2011004459

Chelsea House books are available at special discounts when purchased in bulk quantities for businesses, associations, institutions, or sales promotions. Please call our Special Sales Department in New York at (212) 967-8800 or (800) 322-8755.

You can find Chelsea House on the World Wide Web at http://www.infobaselearning.com

Text design by Erik Lindstrom
Cover design by Alicia Post
Composition by Keith Trego
Cover printed by Yurchak Printing, Landisville, Pa.
Book printed and bound by Yurchak Printing, Landisville, Pa.
Date printed: August 2011
Printed in the United States of America

10 9 8 7 6 5 4 3 2 1

This book is printed on acid-free paper.

CONTENTS

Age of Mass Consumption

In August 1913, at Henry Ford's Highland Park factory in Highland Park, Michigan, history was made. The Model T Ford, the automobile that took America on the road, became the first manufactured product of its kind to come off an automated assembly line.

On that first primitive assembly line, each worker had one specific task to perform. A worker would perform his one task, perhaps something as simple as tightening screw number 86. Then the car would be moved down to the next worker. This continued until the car was completed and ready to come off the assembly line. With that seemingly simple breakthrough, manufacturing, labor relations, and the role of the consumer would never be the same again.

In the words of Bob Casey, the curator for the Henry Ford Museum in Dearborn, Michigan, it was "the most significant technological development of the 20th century."[1] Finally, a system had been developed by which a quality item could be manufactured without using traditional, expensive handcrafting methods. Instead, a process had been created in which interchangeable machine-made parts were added to a product in a logical and time-efficient manner, allowing the finished product to be created in a shorter time than ever before.

In addition, with products coming off assembly lines at faster and faster rates, manufacturers were able to charge less for those products, bringing them within reach of more and more consumers. Automobiles, appliances, and other items once considered luxuries now became available to consumers in quantities and at prices that had been unimaginable just years earlier.

The age of mass consumption had begun. For the first time, products could be manufactured faster than consumers could purchase them. This in turn led to a new emphasis on marketing. Advertising was created to encourage the purchase of products that consumers may or may not have actually known they needed.

It seemed that everybody at all levels of society benefited from the assembly line. Manufacturers' profits were never higher. Workers were earning better wages than ever before. Consumers had more to buy at lower prices than ever before.

Within 20 years of its development, however, doubts were being raised about the effect the automated assembly line had on the individual. Writers began to question the impact that working on an assembly line had on workers who spent their days performing one simple task over and over again, virtually becoming part of the machine. Was this a good thing?

In his 1932 classic novel, *Brave New World*, Aldous Huxley writes of a chilling future in which all time is measured from the first appearance of the Model T. Workers are bred to perform specific tasks: Alphas are designed to be workers of the highest intelligence. Epsilons are bred to be of lesser intelli-

An Assembly Line
of the
Ford Motor Company

Henry Ford's invention of the moving assembly line changed manufacturing forever. The invention not only increased his company's profits and production, but it also lowered prices for consumers and raised worker wages.

gence, to do the most physically demanding tasks. In Huxley's book, the regimented world of the assembly line had spread out to encompass the whole of society, Henry Ford is considered a messianic figure, and individuality is lost in the fast-paced consumer-driven world brought about, in no small part, by Ford and the assembly line.

Moviemakers, as well, began to examine the effects of the assembly line. Films could easily demonstrate to a wide audience the way in which working on an assembly line made workers just part of a vast manufacturing machine. In his 1931 film *À nous la liberté* (Give Us Our Freedom), French director René Clair explored the results of mass production on both workers and consumers. The movie centers on two characters, Louis and Émile, who become friends in prison and meet up years later when Louis gets a job in Émile's phonograph factory. There, Louis finds himself working on an assembly line that is as strictly regimented as a prison. It was "the first film to explore the social ramifications of mass production."[2]

The biggest movie star of the era, silent film genius Charlie Chaplin, took Clair's vision one step further in his 1936 masterpiece, *Modern Times*. In it, after juxtaposing scenes of workers entering a factory with sheep being led to slaughter, Chaplin sets his character, the Little Tramp, to work in a factory producing an unknown item. He is surrounded by vast machinery, equipment that completely dominates him and his fellow workers. In one famous scene, the Little Tramp is caught up in the machinery itself and is swept through a series of cogs and gears—literally becoming a part of the machine.

In a later scene, Chaplin's character goes to work on an automated assembly line, tightening bolts on an unspecified object. As the pace of the line is sped up, the character has to work harder and harder just to keep up with the continuous flow of work. In an effort to improve worker efficiency, automated machines are added to the line to feed the employees as they work, dispensing with the need for a lunch break. What seems ludicrous to the viewer was not far from the truth: Many real-life workers in the early days of the assembly line testified that a trough was placed in front of each worker, to be used instead of taking a bathroom break.

Eventually, the pace of the assembly line becomes too much for Chaplin's character. He goes berserk, unable to stop his body from making the same jerkily repetitive movements he made while tightening bolts. He is taken away from the factory in a wagon and eventually lands in prison, where he finds the peace and quiet he needs to unwind from the regimentation he found in the outside world. By film's end, he has left the city all together and is seen walking down a country road with his girlfriend, looking for a brighter future. In this cinematic master-piece, Chaplin had a definite message he was trying to deliver, one that he articulated in his later film, *The Great Dictator*:

> Machinery that gives us abundance has left us in want. Our knowledge has made us cynical, our cleverness hard and unkind. We think too much and feel too little. More than machinery, we need humanity. More than cleverness, we need kindness and gentleness. Without these qualities, life will be violent, and all will be lost.

And finally, in his 1991 book, *Rivethead: Tales from the Assembly Line*, writer Ben Hamper describes the first time he visited his father at work. His father, just like his father before him, worked on an automobile assembly line.

> After a hundred wrong turns and dead ends, we found my old man down on the trim line. His job was to install windshields using this goofy apparatus with large suction cups that resembled an octopus being crucified. A car would nuzzle up to the old man's work area and he would be wait-ing for it, a cigarette dangling from his lip, his arms wrapped around the windshield contraption as if it might rebel and bolt off for the ocean. Car, windshield. Car, windshield. Car, windshield. . . . This kind of repetition didn't look like any fun at all. . . .
>
> We stood there for forty minutes or so, a miniature life-time, and the pattern never changed. Car, windshield. Car, windshield. Drudgery piled atop drudgery. Cigarette to cigarette. Decades rolling through the rafters, bones turning to dust, stubborn clocks gagging down flesh, another wind-shield, another cigarette. . . . NOTHINGNESS. I wanted to shout at my father, "Do something else!" Do something else or come home with us or flee. . . . DO SOMETHING ELSE! Car, windshield. Car, windshield.[3]

ASSEMBLY LINES THROUGHOUT HISTORY

Although it had its downsides, the automated assembly line had an overwhelmingly positive effect on American society. What may seem odd to us now is just how long it took for the assembly line to be developed. From our perspective, the idea seems ridiculously obvious—instead of having one person manufacture an entire product, say a car, break the product down into smaller parts. Manufacture those, and then assemble the entire product in one continuous action down a moving line. Instead of the worker going to the car, the car goes to the worker. It seems like an easy idea. So why did the creation of the assembly line not take place sooner than 1913?

In fact, history is filled with attempts to manufacture items using just such a process. In ancient China around the year 215 B.C., Emperor Shih Huang Ti ordered that an army be built. But this was to be a terra-cotta army: a collection of nearly 8,000 life-size clay soldiers and horses that would be buried with the emperor upon his death. Each figure had separate body parts that were made at different workshops and were later assembled to make the completed soldiers. Each workshop inscribed its name on the part that it manufactured so that the part's quality could be traced back to the source.

There is also evidence that the ancient Assyrians used a system of bucket elevators called the "chain of pots" to help speed up the manufacturing process. The Great Pyramid of Cheops in Egypt was built in a way not unlike an assembly line. Miners in medieval Europe used a similar system of elevators, as did the Assyrians, and by the time of the Renaissance, engineers had become familiar with at the least the concept of the moving assembly line.

By the fourteenth century, for example, the Venetian Arsenal, Venice's shipyard and naval depot, employed thousands of workers who, at the height of their efficiency, were able to produce one ship a day. They achieved this by using prefabricated parts to assemble and equip their warships. A Spanish visitor to the arsenal in 1436 described the process.

> As one enters the gate, there is a great street on either hand with the sea in the middle, and on one side are windows opening out of the houses of the Arsenal, and the same on the other side. And out came a galley towed by a boat and from the windows they handed out to them, from one the cordage, from another the bread, from another the arms, and from another the ballistas and mortars, and so from all sides everything that was required. And when the galley had reached the end of the street, all the men required were on board, together with the complement of oars, and she was fully equipped from end to end.[4]

And, indeed, what may have been the first powered-roller conveyer system was introduced as early as 1804 by the British navy's automatic production of hardtack, or biscuits, using a steam engine to power its rollers.

Still, those early attempts at using an automated system to increase production were still a long way from the assembly line as devised by Henry Ford. Throughout the nineteenth century, there were manufacturers and inventors who worked hard to solve the problem of how to manufacture products in large quantities while at the same time keeping the quality high. But there were five problems that had to be solved before the assembly line could become a reality. The problems were these: labor and how to organize it, how to create interchangeable parts, how to devise single-function machines, what was the best way to design the factory space, and finally, how to move parts easily from one place to another. It was Henry Ford who finally put the pieces of the puzzle together, but as with most inventions, it was the work of many before him that allowed him to get there.

Interchangeability

B efore there could be an assembly line, before manufacturers could start producing products in large numbers, it was necessary to find a way to achieve interchangeability. But what exactly is interchangeability, and what are interchangeable parts?

Interchangeable parts are parts that for all intents and purposes are identical. They are made to exacting specifications so that, because they are virtually identical, each one will fit into any machine of the same type. For example, each screw number 86, which attached part A to part B in a Model T, was the exact same size and would attach part A to part B in every Model T that was made.

With interchangeability, it became easier to assemble new devices, as well as to repair existing devices. Both the time and skill necessary to manufacture or repair items were minimized. With interchangeability, manufacturers were on their way to achieving the means of mass production—the production of large quantities of a standardized item.

Before the eighteenth century, however, the goal of interchangeability seemed a distant dream. Items were still being made one at a time, by hand, each one slightly different from the other. Guns, for example, were made by trained gunsmiths one at a time, each one an individual work of art. Although these items were well-crafted works of art, there were drawbacks. If, for example, any part of the weapon needed to be replaced, the owner could not go down to the local store and buy a new part.

Instead, the entire weapon either had to be sent back to the gunsmith for repair or thrown away to be replaced by another weapon. The system took enormous amounts of time and money. As the world's population grew, and more and more items were required for that growing population, it became apparent that things would have to change.

THE UNIFORMITY SYSTEM

It was the French who made the first steps toward finding a way to manufacture interchangeable parts. In 1765, French general Jean-Baptiste de Gribeauval began the quest in order to keep the French military competitive and to create a more rational system of French armaments. To do so, he felt it would be necessary to introduce to the army weapons built to one standard with standardized parts.

Such a system, he believed, would allow for complete interchangeability within the military itself. Parts of guns and larger artillery weapons could be interchanged, while the arms themselves could be interchanged just as easily as soldiers could be switched from one position to another. The system was known in France for years as *le système Gribeauval*.

At the same time, French gunsmith Honoré Blanc began to work out a system of interchangeability on his own. What he wanted to do was find a way to manufacture gun parts using allowable tolerances. This means that the parts were not perfectly interchangeable. But they *were* close enough so that any part from a specific production run could fit and function in any gun manufactured to allow for the same system of tolerances.

Blanc demonstrated his system in front of a committee of scientists, proving to them that his muskets could be assembled from a pile of parts selected at random. While scientists as well as the French military saw the immediate advantage to his system, his fellow craftspeople were not so receptive. Their objection? If Blanc could manufacture guns more quickly and cheaply than they could, their status as makers of individual fine guns, as well as their very job security, could be threatened.

So instead, Blanc turned for encouragement to the American ambassador to France, Thomas Jefferson. Jefferson, an Enlightenment man whose interests ranged from politics to government to architecture to horticulture, immediately grasped the system's potential. With it, he felt, America could be freed from having to purchase weapons from Europe and could quickly build its own system of weapons manufacture.

In 1785, Jefferson sent a letter explaining the system to John Jay, who at the time was secretary of foreign affairs:

> An improvement is made here in the construction of the musket which it may be interesting to Congress to know, should they at any time propose to procure any. It consists in the making of every part of them so exactly alike that what belongs to any one may be used for every other musket in the magazine. The government here has examined and approved the method, and is establishing a large manufactory for this purpose. As yet the inventor [Honoré Blanc] has only completed the lock of the musket on this plan. He will proceed immediately to have the barrel, stock and their parts executed in the same way. Supposing it might be useful to the U.S. I went to the workman. He presented me with the parts

of 50 locks taken to pieces and arranged in compartments. I put several together myself taking pieces at hazard as they came to hand, and they fitted in the most perfect manner. The advantages of this, when arms need repair, are evident.[1]

Jefferson was so enthused about the idea that he tried to convince Blanc to move himself and his operations to the United States, but to no avail. Instead, Jefferson turned to the American secretary of war with the idea, and when he returned to the United States later that year as the new secretary of state, to America's first president, George Washington.

Washington approved the idea. America's ties to the French military were still strong, so it is not surprising that Washington would embrace the new "French" idea. In 1798, a contract was issued to the famous inventor Eli Whitney to build 12,000 muskets. It seemed an unlikely feat, but then, Eli Whitney was a rather unlikely man.

ELI WHITNEY

Eli Whitney was born on December 8, 1765, to Eli Whitney Sr., a well-to-do farmer, and his wife, Elizabeth Fay, who died when Eli was 11. Showing an early talent for business and manufacturing, by the time Eli was 14 years old he was operating a successful nail manufacturing concern based in his father's workshop during the Revolutionary War.

Eli Whitney's stepmother opposed his going to college, so he worked on a farm and as a schoolteacher to save up some money. Later, accepted by Yale, where he planned to study law, he found himself short of money once again and went to Georgia to work, entering into business with Phineas Miller, a Yale graduate and fellow migrant from Connecticut. Whitney's next venture would be the one that made him a household name.

The invention was the cotton gin (1793), the idea for which he is best known today. The gin was a mechanical device that

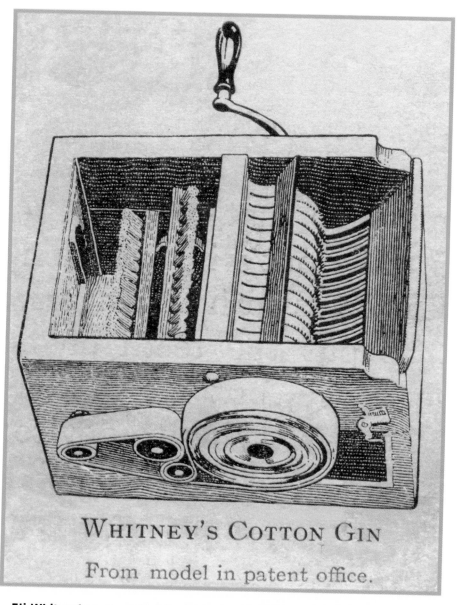

WHITNEY'S COTTON GIN

From model in patent office.

Eli Whitney's cotton gin introduced a faster, less labor-intensive way of processing cotton. Because it no longer took hours to remove the seeds from the crop, southern plantation owners could increase their harvest, make more money, and acquire additional slave laborers.

removed the seeds from cotton, speeding up a process that, until then, had been extremely labor intensive. The cotton gin revolutionized the way in which cotton was harvested: In 1793 total cotton production was 180,000 pounds (81,647 kilograms); by 1810 it had risen to 93 million tons (84.4 million metric tons).

Because cotton was once again profitable to grow, slavery, which had begun to decrease in importance, was once again the prime source of labor throughout the South where cotton was grown. Indeed, it could be said that without the cotton gin, slavery might have faded away completely and the tragedy of the Civil War might never have come to pass.

Perhaps surprisingly, Whitney did not earn the financial fortune he had hoped for from his gin. Years of patent battles and litigation left him nearly bankrupt by the late 1790s. Fortunately for him, however, another opportunity to make his fortune would soon appear.

The U.S. government, which was still finding its footing after the Revolution, recognized the need to have the ability to protect itself from foreign threat. The War Department issued contracts for the manufacture of muskets for the new army, and Eli Whitney, who had never built a weapon in his life, received a contract in January 1798 to deliver between 10,000 and 15,000 muskets in 1800. The contract could save him from financial ruin. But would he be able to deliver what he promised?

It would have been a tall order even for someone with experience in weapons manufacturing. But Whitney promised the War Department that he would use new technologies such as interchangeability to help him achieve his goals Indeed, for years Whitney, his supporters, and some historians claimed that he invented what became known as the American system of manufacturing—the use of power machinery, interchangeable parts, and the division of labor—that would power the

Industrial Revolution and lead to the automated assembly line. The historical record, however, shows that was not quite the case.

Indeed, as historian David A. Hounshell points out, it was not until nearly 10 months after receiving the contract that Whitney began to promote what he called the "uniformity principle."[2] Why the sudden need to promote interchangeability? By the middle of 1800, when the contract was to have been completed, Whitney had yet to manufacture or deliver a single weapon. By using his quest for interchangeability as his excuse, he was able to buy himself additional time.

It would take him another nine years to deliver the muskets. However, the promise of building them with interchangeable parts proved to be a pipe dream. Hounshell describes the story of Eli Whitney and armory production as "the story of a man who espoused the two principles that lay behind the system—interchangeability and mechanization—but who never understood, much less developed, its basic principles . . . not [a] heroic innovator. . . . Whitney was a publicist of mechanized, interchangeable parts manufacture, not a creator."[3]

Yet Whitney's fame helped spur others on to achieve what he could not. Clockmaker Eli Terry created what historian Diane Muir called "the world's first complex machine mass-produced from interchangeable parts."[4] The "complex machine" was Terry's pillar-and-scroll clock, which began to roll off the production line in 1814. These clocks, though, were made of wooden parts. Making a machine with moving parts mass-produced from metal would prove to be a much more difficult task.

It would be up to another arms manufacturer, Simeon North, to create the world's first machine capable of shaping metal (work that previously, as under Eli Whitney, had to be done by hand, shaping each piece with a file). This machine probably became operable around 1816. By 1832, both Simeon North and fellow manufacturer John Hall were able to mass-produce complex machines with moving parts—guns, to be specific—using a system that required the use of rough-forged parts.

This meant that a milling machine was used to mill the parts to a near-correct size, and those parts were then filed down by hand with the aid of filing jigs, which guided the workman's file and designed stencils with up to a dozen holes that helped to bore in the exact places. The parts were not perfectly interchangeable—nothing made and finished by hand could be. But they were getting close.

It was at John Hall's Rifle Works, located at Harpers Ferry, Virginia (today's West Virginia), where two important aspects of manufacturing technology came together. It was there that the concept of interchangeability combined with the idea that machines could be used to make things as good or even *better* than could be made by hand. The result of this combination, as Hounshell points out, was the method of production that has come to be known as the "American system of manufactures." Although, as he adds, it might be more appropriate to call it the "armory system" or "armory practice," since it was in the manufacture of weapons, or armory, that it came into being.

Indeed, it was the U.S. government arsenal, known as the Springfield Armory, that played a crucial part not only in the development of a practical, mechanized system of uniform firearms manufacture but in the passing along of information about that system throughout the country. As we have seen, the military took the lead in the search for interchangeable parts, simply because it was easier to replace broken firearm parts rather than attempt to repair them on the battlefield.

Arms makers such as Samuel Colt, who initially relied on the government to purchase his patented revolvers, used the technology and techniques they learned to be able to mass-produce weapons for the general public. The parts of Colt's weapons were not interchangeable—the machine-made parts were still filed down and fitted while still warm by workmen. After being assembled, the gun's major parts were stamped with serial

When Samuel Colt first entered the arms industry, he could manufacture only a limited number of revolvers. Colt later integrated machines into his production methods and was able to expand his business to sell uniform, mass-produced revolvers to the general public.

numbers, and the gun was taken apart to allow the parts to cool and harden. After that, the parts with the same numbers would be reassembled and fitted to make the completed revolver.

Unlike the muskets being manufactured at the Springfield Armory, Colt's revolvers were not interchangeable. Even so, Colt's armory proved that mechanization on a wider scale than ever before attempted was practical, and it became the standard from which other inventors learned. It also became a showcase for America's rapidly growing technological prowess.

FOREIGN INSPECTION

Two Englishmen, Joseph Whitworth and George Wallis, came to the United States in 1853 as commissioners to the second Exhibition of the Industries of All Nations, held in New York City's Crystal Palace. The pair traveled throughout the East Coast of the United States, visiting factories of all sorts. They were impressed by what they saw, praising "the eagerness with which they [the Americans] call in the aid of machinery in almost every department of industry."[5] Not surprisingly, it was the work being done at the Springfield Armory that most impressed the two.

The British Select Committee on Small Arms sent John Anderson and his fellow committeemen to learn more. Earlier, Anderson had visited Samuel Colt's London armory and had been impressed by what he saw. Anderson said:

> This manufactory is reduced to an almost perfect system; a pistol being composed of a certain number of distinct pieces, and as each piece when finished is the result of a number of operations . . . and each operation being performed by a special machine made on purpose, many of these machines requiring hardly any skill from the attendant beyond knowing how to fasten and unfasten the article, the setting and adjusting of the machine being performed by skilled workmen; but when once the machine is properly set it will produce thousands.[6]

He was even more impressed by what he saw at the Springfield Armory. He and his committee went to the main arsenal and randomly picked one musket made each year from 1844 to 1853. Those muskets were then taken apart and the corresponding parts of each musket put into separate boxes. The parts were then mixed up, and Anderson's committee was allowed to select parts from each box at random. Those parts were given over to a workman, who, using only a simple screwdriver, rebuilt the muskets "as quickly as though they had been English muskets whose parts had carefully been kept separate."[7]

Anderson reported back to his government that interchangeability of parts (at least when it came to arms manufacturing) had been achieved. The British, he advised, would be wise to adopt the American system as quickly as possible. Otherwise, he felt, American-built weapons would soon be exported in large numbers to England, possibly damaging the British arms industry.

His prediction came true. By and large, British gun makers refused to adopt the American system, and American weapons began to be exported to England in greater and greater numbers. And while the quality of the American weapons may not have been as high as the guns that were handmade by the British, their lower prices more than helped to make up for that.

The Americans had proved that while interchangeability was not yet perfected, it was already "good enough" that lower-priced, mass-produced guns could compete with traditional hand-built ones in terms of quality. Now that interchangeability had been achieved (if not perfected) in gun manufacturing, it would be interesting to see what business would take it to the next step.

The Sewing Machine

C uriously, if it was the gun manufacturers who took the first steps toward the modern assembly line through their use of interchangeable parts, it would be the sewing machine industry that took it to the next level. In an 1890 article titled "What the World Owes to the Sewing Machine Workman" in the *Sewing Machine Advance*, the writer boasts of the accomplishment:

> The gun-maker's tools were carried to the sewing machine manufactory, but as the demand grew for a better quality of work these tools were improved until we find the sewing machine now in possession of the improved milling machine, the perfected screw machine . . . a complete system of "jig" working, and a system of measuring by decimals; often extending to tens of thousandths and frequently beyond the ten thousandths. . . . Gauge work is an outgrowth from a rude

system that originated in the armories, but has been perfected and systematized in the sewing machine manufactory.[1]

But that perfect and systematized process did not occur overnight.

It had been Samuel Colt who told the British Parliament that it was not just guns that could be made by machine—anything could. By adopting and refining the production technology developed by Colt and others, sewing machine manufacturers proved that a larger, more complicated machine, such as a sewing machine, could also be manufactured by machine.

There were problems along the way. The sewing machine industry was at constant war with itself, as litigation over patents kept any one company from achieving dominance over the others and threatened to drive the entire industry to ruin. The answer to the fighting was what is considered to be the first important pooling arrangement (a resource or service shared by a group of people) in American history, known as the Great Sewing Machine Combination.

Elias Howe contributed his 1846 patent for a grooved eye-pointed needle and lock-stitch-forming shuttle. Allen B. Wilson of the Wheeler and Wilson Manufacturing Company granted use of his patented cloth-feeding mechanism. I.M. Singer provided a number of his patents as well. Members of the pool could use any of those patents at no charge, as could other manufacturers willing to pay a licensing fee of $15 per machine.

This pool gave access to nearly every important part of the sewing machine process to anyone willing to pay the fee. This had the effect of opening up the industry to newcomers and allowed established businesses to expand their operations without fear of costly legal battles.

A CHANGING OF THE GUARD

The company that sold the most sewing machines through 1867 was the Wheeler and Wilson Manufacturing Company.

Skilled workers handcrafted unique Wheeler and Wilson sewing machines for the public, but the product did not succeed until the process was mechanized. Mechanization increased production and allowed the company to hire unskilled employees at cheaper wages, making the sewing machine more available to the general public at a lower cost.

It began manufacturing them in the classic way, painstakingly building them one machine at a time, rather than making all the parts and then assembling them. As *Scientific American* magazine noted, "The price of one all complete is $125; every machine is made under the eye of the inventor at the Company's machine shop, Watertown, Connecticut."[2]

Each piece was unique and handcrafted to the company's exacting specifications. Doing it this way, the company produced 4,591 sewing machines in 1857. Three years later, in

1860, its production had risen to 25,102 machines. What was the difference?

In 1855, William H. Perry had joined the company. Knowledgeable in the techniques used at Samuel Colt's armory, Perry was determined to demonstrate that sewing machines could be built in the same way. He was right. A new factory was built in Bridgeport, Connecticut, using the latest technologies, and by 1862, the company had the capacity to build nearly 30,000 sewing machines per year.

The company boasted that because of the accuracy it had achieved in building parts, the machines could be assembled "as is" without the need of filing to hone their accuracy. Taking the lessons he had learned at the Colt armory, William Perry proved that larger, even more complicated machines such as a sewing machine could be assembled the same way as the simpler gun and musket. By 1872, 174,088 Wheeler and Wilson sewing machines were leaving the Bridgeport factory.

Curiously though, there was one essential part of the sewing machine that could not be made using the American system—the needle. Making a sewing needle was still a multistep process, from cutting the wire all the way to the polishing of the finished product. And because they were made by hand by skilled laborers, the cost was shockingly high. Even as late as the 1880s, while much of the handwork had been eliminated by the use of machines, each and every needle was still straightened with a hammer on an anvil.

There were other sewing machine companies as well. Some, such as Willcox & Gibbs, had been using the armory system from the beginning with great success. But the best-known sewing machine company in the country today, the company whose very name is synonymous with sewing machines, resisted the new manufacturing ideas for as long as it could.

The company, of course, is the Singer Manufacturing Company. The earliest sewing machines made by Singer were large and heavy, weighing more than 125 pounds (57 kg). In

Although Singer's handcrafted sewing machine was more expensive than any other machine, the company's successful marketing campaign made it popular with consumers. As demand increased, Singer was forced to adopt the armory method to improve its product's quality and increase supply.

addition, unlike the machines made by Wheeler and Wilson, each individual piece was still carefully filed and polished to fit the final assembly. Each sewing machine was proudly "produced by hand at the bench."[3] Yet, despite the high price and low production numbers of Singer sewing machines, sales continued to climb.

The Singer Manufacturing Company, while initially resisting the American system of manufactures, seized on a way to find consumers willing to pay a high price for a sewing machine: advertising. The Singer Company was famous for its marketing program, which used trained women to demonstrate to consumers the capabilities of the sewing machine. It also advertised in newspapers and magazines, with large ads extolling the high quality of the Singer.

Indeed, the company stated that "a large part of our success we attribute to our numerous advertisements and publications. To insure success only two things are required: 1st to have the best machines and 2nd to let the public know it."[4] Years later, Henry Ford would seize on this concept to make his Model T Ford the best-selling car in America.

That high quality came at a high price, however. The company believed that it was only through hand finishing done by highly skilled workers that such product quality could be achieved and maintained. To help the consumer purchase the more expensive machine, the company introduced the idea of the "hire-purchase system," or, as we would call it, installment payments. This allowed the consumer to pay for his or her sewing machine in small monthly payments, "hiring" the machine until it was completely paid for.

Singer's sales continued to rise, aided by the introduction of the first sewing machine designed strictly for home use. But the company still resisted the armory system, relying for the next 15 years on using large numbers of workmen to finish pieces for assembly. By 1863, sales reached 21,000 machines annually.

Problems emerged, perhaps due to the large number of machines being manufactured under the old system, and complaints began to rise about the quality of the machines. It became clear to the company's leadership that manufacturing in such large numbers without the extensive use of machines simply was not working.

The company slowly began to switch over to the American system. New machines were brought in; gears were made by automatic gear-cutting machines. By 1873, Singer had fully switched over to the American system of making interchangeable parts by tools and machinery. As historian David A. Hounshell points out, it was because of Singer's rising sewing machine sales—up to nearly 250,000 by 1873—that the company was forced to find a way to increase production and improve quality. The American system of manufactures proved to be the way.

It was not easy. Learning to manufacture the close-fitting, interchangeable parts needed to assemble the high-quality machines that the company had built its reputation on was a slow process. Determined to make the system work, Singer pushed ahead, and by 1880, biographer John Scott was able to write that Singer's Elizabethport factory "is believed to be the most complete, systematic, and best-equipped in the world [and] . . . is believed to be the largest establishment in the world devoted to the manufacture of a single article."[5]

The company had still not achieved absolute interchangeability; workers were still needed in small numbers to file some parts down to fit. But it was close. And it had become apparent to manufacturers of all kinds of products that achieving absolute interchangeability would be essential for mass production. Samuel Colt, the Springfield Armory, and sewing machine manufacturers had begun the process. The industry that would take manufacturing to the next level produced transportation for the masses, but it was not a car. It was a product that you probably have sitting in your garage at home. It was the bicycle.

The Bicycle

In David A. Hounshell's 1984 book, *From the American System to Mass Production, 1800–1932*, he opens his chapter on bicycle manufacturing with the following quote:

> Another event having an effect on the designing and manufacturing of machinery entirely unlooked for at the time of its inception was the manufacture of the bicycle. This event brought out the capabilities of the American mechanic as nothing else had ever done. It demonstrated to the world that he and his kind were capable of designing and making special machinery, tools, fixtures, and devices for economic manufacturing in a manner truly marvelous; and has led to the installation of the interchangeable system of manufacture in a thousand and one shops where it was formerly thought to be impractical.[1]

This quote was taken from Joseph Woodworth's 1907 book, *American Tool Making and Interchangeable Manufacturing.* What is interesting to note is that even at that early date, Woodworth was already aware of the impact that bicycle manufacturing had had throughout the country. What he did not yet know was the impact that was still to come. That next stop would be a nearly unending stream of Model T Fords rolling off an automated assembly line.

EARLY BICYCLES

Today, like so many other inventions, the bicycle seems far too simple an idea to have actually been invented. But it was not until 1817 that the first bicycle was introduced to the public in Mannheim, Germany, the creation of Baron Karl von Drais. It was not quite a bicycle in the way we know bicycles now. To make it move, the rider sat astride a wooden frame supported by two wheels and pushed the bicycle along using both feet.

It was in the early 1860s that Pierre Michaux and Pierre Lallement took bicycle design in a new direction with the addition of a mechanical crank drive with pedals on an enlarged front wheel. It was in this form that the high-wheel, or "ordinary," bicycle first appeared in the United States, where Albert A. Pope of Boston saw it presented at the 1876 Centennial Exhibition in Philadelphia.

It was love at first sight. Pope traveled to England to learn how the bicycles were made and, upon returning home, began selling imported British cycles. Two years later, he made a deal with the Weed Sewing Machine Company of Hartford, Connecticut, to manufacture his own American version of the British bike. With that, the Columbia, the new American bicycle, began the age of the bicycle in America.

It might seem unusual that Pope turned to a sewing machine company to manufacture bicycles. Recall that by 1878, the Singer Company had, through its use of the armory system, become the predominant sewing machine manufacturer in the

Many of the machines used in manufacturing could be adapted to make other products, such as bicycles. Albert Pope manufactured his bicycle, the Columbia, in a factory that had previously produced sewing machines and rifles. Pope would later adapt these same machines for automobile production.

nation. Because of this, other sewing machine companies were faced with a difficult choice. They could go out of business, or they could start to manufacture other items. The Weed Sewing Machine Company chose to do the latter.

There was another reason why Pope turned to the Weed Sewing Machine Company. Although the company was not nearly as successful as Singer, it did have one thing that Singer did not: In 1875, Weed had moved its operations into the former armorer Sharps Manufacturing Company plant, using the same machines that had made interchangeable parts for rifles and adapting them to make interchangeable parts for sewing machines. Now, those same machines would be used to make bicycles. (Years later, Pope would use the same factory to make automobiles, proof of the nearly direct line from weaponry to sewing machines to bicycles to cars.)

Interestingly, the same machinery used for manufacturing sewing machines could be used to manufacture high-wheel bicycles. There was, however, one exception: ball bearings. The extensive use of ball bearings in bicycles called for new machines to manufacture those ball bearings. Not only were ball bearings used in bicycles, those same ball bearings were soon found in most new machines used to manufacture *other* items.

Although it had become relatively easy to manufacture the separate parts of a bicycle, assembling them was another matter. Back in 1853, it had been possible to put together an entire Springfield musket in just three minutes. But to assemble and adjust one single big bicycle wheel took 20 times as long.

Everything had to be done by hand. One assembler was needed just to string the hub and rim together with machine-made spokes. Then, once all the spokes were put in, more workmen were needed to "true" the wheel—painstakingly tightening and loosening each of the individual spokes. It is little wonder that even after expanding his plant and hiring additional workers, by 1881 Pope could make only 50 bicycles per day.

As long as it was the high-wheel bicycle that was in fashion, however, it seemed likely that sales would grow only so much. The bicycles were not particularly safe, and riding was largely limited to the most daring of men. That all changed in 1887 when the "safety" bike, the bicycle as we know it today with two level wheels, was introduced. With that, the entire family could enjoy bike riding, and sales exploded.

With the need for more and more bicycles, new technologies were developed to make the safety bicycle possible. Electric resistance welding, which allowed metals to be fused by the direct application of electricity, was one such technology that would have wide-ranging applications. Because the new safety bicycle, unlike the high-wheel bicycle, required a chain and two sprockets, as well as an extra axle and set of ball bearings and a crank hanger to support them, the safety required twice as much framing material. Designers and engineers worked together to find ways to lower the weight of the safety (originally between 40 and 70 pounds, or 18 and 32 kg) down to between 20 and 27 pounds (9 and 12 kg)!

MEANWHILE IN THE WEST

Pope was not alone in building bicycles. Many other bicycle manufacturers sprang up on the East Coast. Most, like Pope,

MARKETING THE BICYCLE

The Singer Manufacturing Company made good use of advertising to sell its products. But as Ross Petty points out in his article "Peddling the Bicycle in the 1890s: Mass Marketing Shifts into High Gear," it was the bicycle that was the first expensive durable luxury item to be truly mass marketed throughout the United States.

It has been estimated that in 1902 for example, manufacturers and retailers spent nearly $7 million in advertising. During the 1890s, it is thought that nearly 10 percent of all newspaper and magazine advertising in the United States was bicycle related. Early advertisements were used to praise the mechanical and engineering features of Columbia's latest bicycle. Then, in later advertisements, after the company had established the quality of its bicycles, images were used that illustrated the effortless speed, almost like flying, that one achieved with bicycles, as well as their ease of use for women.

built in the same factories that had originally made guns and sewing machines. In the West, though, things were different. Bicycles were made by carriage and wagon makers, toy makers, and agricultural equipment manufacturers, or by brand-new businesses.

Because they rose from different industries, production techniques in the West differed from those in the East. It was from them, especially from the Western Wheel Works, that the movement began away from forging equipment (equipment used to beat and hammer metal), which required a large amount of boring (making a hole), drilling, and waste, to using sheet metal and simply punching and pressing out the parts needed. It is true that these parts were not as strong as those forged in the East. The western manufacturers argued,

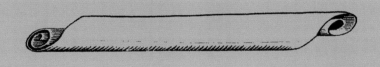

Another effective technique used to promote bicycles was in the use of artistic posters. This period was the heyday of poster art, and bicycle companies eagerly sought out the finest artists of the day. Prizes were offered: In an 1895 contest held by the Pope Manufacturing Company, prizes included a Columbia bicycle with a value of $100 for fourth place, and the same bicycle plus cash for the winners of third, second, and first place. The winner of the first-place prize of $250 and a bicycle? Renowned poster artist Maxfield Parrish, who defeated more than 400 other artists to claim the win.

By showing that advertising could effectively be used both to introduce and sell a new product to the public, bicycle companies helped to open the way to the wide world of advertising we have today.

Popular demand drove the growth of the bicycle industry, and new manufacturers established themselves throughout the country. Factories in the West that had previously created wagons, toys, or agricultural equipment did not produce a high-quality product, but they were deemed "good enough" for the consumer. Above, women work in a bicycle factory.

though, that they were "good enough" to make a high-quality bicycle. Is it possible that the forged parts made in the East were "too good"?

By 1897, the bubble had burst in the bicycle boom and sales began to drop sharply. The fad, like so many other fads, was over. Although the bicycle would never again achieve the same popularity in the United States as it did in the late nineteenth century, it did serve as a critical step on the road to the assembly line, and it helped to bring about the birth of the automobile. And in its own way, as W.J. McGee wrote in his 1898 article "Fifty Years of American Science" in the *Atlantic Monthly*, it was one of the great inventions. McGee explained:

> Invented in France, it long remained a toy or a vain luxury. Redevised in this country, it inspired inventors and captivated manufacturers and native genius made it a practical machine for the multitude. . . . Typical too, is the bicycle in its effect on national character. It first aroused invention, next stimulated commerce, and then developed individuality, judgment, and prompt decision on the part of its users more rapidly and completely than any other device . . . the bicycle is the easy leader of other machines in shaping the mind of its rider, and transforming itself and its rider into a single thing. Better than other results is this . . . that the bicycle has broken the barrier of . . . differentiation between the sexes. So, weighed by its effect on body and mind as well as on material progress, this device must be classed as one of the world's great inventions.[2]

FROM BICYCLES TO AUTOMOBILES

The extraordinary popularity of bicycles, although short-lived, had several interesting side effects. Support grew both to allow bicycles to be classified as a transportation vehicle, legal to operate in cities, as well as to build good roads to operate them on. It was this very movement that led to both state and federal involvement in the building of roads and highways throughout the country.

Roads, however, needed to be driven on. As early as 1895, Albert A. Pope had predicted the birth of the "motor-carriage." He also argued that good roads, which he and other bicyclists had been fighting for, would be crucial: "The day of the horse is already beginning to wane, and as soon as the practical motor-carriage can be had by men of moderate means we must have good roads, not only in and about cities, but throughout the entire country."[3]

Pope was so convinced that the "motor-carriage" was the next logical step after the bicycle that in 1895 he hired Hiram Percy Maxim to begin building test versions of automobiles. Nearly 40 years later, in his book *Horseless Carriage Days*, Maxim claimed that he had conceived the idea for an automobile in 1892, while riding his bicycle. Maxim explained:

> I saw [transportation] emerging from a crude state in which mankind was limited to the railroad, to the horse, or to shank's mare. The bicycle was just becoming popular and it represented a very significant advance, I felt. Here I was covering the distance between Salem and Lynn on a bicycle. Here was a revolutionary change in transportation. My bicycle was propelled at a respectable speed by a mechanism operated by my muscles. It carried me over a lonely country road in the middle of the night, covering the distance in considerably less than an hour. A horse and carriage would require nearly two hours. A railroad train would require half an hour, and it would carry me only from station to station. And I must conform to its time-table, which was not always convenient.[4]

In his memoir, Maxim went on to explain why it took so long for industry to begin manufacturing automobiles: "The reason why we did not build mechanical road vehicles before this, was the bicycle had not yet come in numbers and had not directed men's minds to the possibilities of independent long-distance travel over the ordinary highway. We thought the railroad was good enough."[5]

But, as is so often the case, one invention, one idea such as the bicycle, leads to other inventions, other ideas, other possibilities. In other words, the bicycle "created a new demand which it was beyond the ability of the railroad to supply. Then it came about that the bicycle could not satisfy the demand which it had created. A mechanically propelled vehicle was wanted instead of a foot-propelled one, and we know that the automobile was the answer."[6]

The bicycle, the first personal form of transportation that did not rely on a horse to propel it, had ignited the desire for better, faster, automated modes of personal transportation. With the introduction of the automobile, that desire would be fulfilled.

The Early Days of the Automobile Industry

Consider these figures. In the United States in 1910, there were 19,000 people for every car. Just 10 years later, that ratio had changed radically. In 1920, there were 11 people for every car in the nation. And today, with well over 250 million motorized passenger vehicles registered in the United States alone (including automobiles, SUVs, pickup trucks, and other trucks), nearly one vehicle per person, it is hard to imagine a world without them.

But again, as with most other inventions, the first car did not just magically appear on the roadway. It was a process of discovery, of one step leading to another and then to another. It would take many steps to get to Detroit, Henry Ford, and the assembly line. The first step, surprisingly enough, took place in China, in the year 1672.

EARLY ATTEMPTS

It is indeed possible that the first self-propelled vehicle was designed by Father Ferdinand Verbiest (1623–1688), a Flemish Jesuit missionary living in China during the time of the Ch'ing dynasty.

An accomplished mathematician and astronomer (he designed the Beijing Ancient Observatory), Verbiest also experimented with steam. Around 1672, he designed, as a toy for the Kangxi Emperor, a steam-powered vehicle, which he described in his book *Astronomia Europea*. While no evidence exists that the vehicle, designed to be only about 25 inches (65 centimeters) long, was ever built, Verbiest did have access to the finest Chinese craftspeople, so it is indeed possible that his "car" was the first ever built.

It did not take long before full-size steam-powered vehicles were being built. In 1770 or 1771, Frenchman Nicholas-Joseph Cugnot demonstrated a steam-driven artillery tractor, and by 1801 Englishman Richard Trevithick was driving a full-size vehicle in Camborne.

Steam-powered vehicles such as this were popular for a time, and improvements such as hand brakes, multispeed transmissions, and better steering helped to make them even more so. They became so successful in Great Britain that they were even used as mass transit. But a backlash soon kicked in as people complained about the noise and danger of having such "speedy" vehicles on roads already crowded with horse-drawn vehicles.

In 1865, Great Britain passed the Locomotive Act, which required that all self-powered vehicles on public roads throughout the United Kingdom be preceded by a man walking on foot, waving a red flag, and blowing a horn to warn everybody of the oncoming "danger." Needless to say, this law killed any further automobile development in Britain through the rest of the nineteenth century. (The law was finally repealed in 1896, although the red flag requirement was removed in 1878.)

In 1789, Oliver Evans received a patent for his Oruktor Amphibolos, a land-sea dredger designed for the Philadelphia Board of Health. The Oruktor Amphibolos was the first self-powered vehicle to receive a U.S. patent, but it remained unused and was eventually sold for parts.

The first "automobile" patent granted in the United States went to inventor Oliver Evans in 1789 for a steam-carriage design. The vehicle, known as the Oruktor Amphibolos (Amphibious Digger), was built in 1805 on commission from the Philadelphia Board of Health. The vehicle was designed to travel on wheels on land and by paddle wheel in water, but it seems unlikely that it ever actually moved at all. After sitting idly for years on a Philadelphia dock, it was sold for parts. It would take the development of the internal combustion engine to make self-powered vehicles at all practical.

INTERNAL COMBUSTION ENGINES

There were problems inherent with steam engines. They had a tendency to blow up, for one thing. In addition, a huge amount of fuel was required just to keep the engine boiling. To travel any distance at all proved to be impractical. So for years, European engineers worked to develop an engine that would be both safer and more efficient. The answer was the internal combustion engine, an engine in which the fuel is burned, or combusted, within the engine itself. (By comparison, in a steam engine, the fuel is burned in a space kept separate from the engine.)

Experiments had begun as early as 1806, when Swiss engineer François Isaac de Rivaz built an internal combustion engine fueled by a mixture of hydrogen and oxygen. Later, in 1826, Samuel Brown tested a hydrogen-fueled internal combustion engine by using it to power a vehicle up a hill in London.

It was not until 1876, though, that German engineer Nikolaus August Otto invented the four-stroke motor that we know today. In it, a piston was packed into a hollow cylinder. The piston was then attached to a rod. That rod was connected to a crankshaft, which would, in turn, run the wheels of the vehicle.

A four-stroke engine consists of, logically, four strokes. In the first, called the intake stroke, the piston is at the top of the cylinder. When the crankshaft is turned, the piston moves down the cylinder. That, in turn, sucks a mixture of fuel and air into the cylinder through the intake valve.

The second stroke, called the compression stroke, is the upward movement of the piston with the intake valve closed. This compresses the mixture of fuel and air. As the piston nears the top of the cylinder, the pressure causes a spark. That spark, in turn, creates a small explosion of the highly combustible air and fuel mixture. The explosion drives the piston down again, in a third stroke known as the combustion stroke.

The final stroke, the fourth stroke, is called the exhaust stroke. It is another upward movement of the piston. But this time, instead of an intake valve, an exhaust valve opens up, and the built-up gasses are forced out of the cylinder. Then,

(continues on page 42)

ELECTRIC CARS

In these days of high energy prices and renewed interest in hybrid vehicles, it might be surprising to note that electric cars have been around nearly as long as cars themselves have been around.

Many have laid claim to inventing the electric vehicle, including Ányos Jedlik, the Hungarian inventor of the electric motor; Vermont blacksmith Thomas Davenport; Professor Sibrandus Stratingh of Groningen, the Netherlands; and Scotsmen Robert Davidson and Robert Anderson. Then, with improvements in battery technology, including contributions by Gaston Planté of France in 1865, as well as fellow Frenchman Camille Faure in 1881, electric cars began to flourish in Europe. Switzerland, lacking in fossil fuels, jumped on the new technology, resulting in the nation's electrification of its railway network.

In England, Thomas Parker successfully electrified the London Underground (subway) system, as well as overhead trams in Liverpool and Birmingham, and claimed to have built a working electric car as early as 1884. Before internal combustion engines were in common use, it was electric automobiles that were setting speed and distance records: Camille Jenatzy broke the 62-mile-per-hour (100-kilometer-per-hour) speed barrier on April 29, 1889, in his rocket-shaped vehicle the *Jamais Contente*, which hit a top speed of 65.79 miles per hour (105.88 kph).

By 1895, American automakers were beginning to take a look at electric cars themselves, after A.L. Ryker introduced the first electric tricycle to the United States. Interest rapidly increased, and in 1897, electric vehicles were being used commercially as a fleet of New York City taxis, built by the Electric Carriage and Wagon Company of Philadelphia. Electric cars for individuals were being built as well, by companies such as Anthony Electric, Baker, Columbia, Anderson, Edison, Studebaker, Riker, and others.

Indeed, by 1917, the first gasoline-electric hybrid car was built by the Woods Motor Vehicle Company of Chicago. The car, though, turned

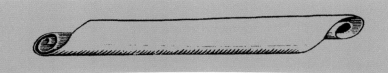

out to be a failure, proving to be too slow for its price and too difficult to service.

Still, compared to both steam-powered vehicles and the early gasoline-powered cars, electric cars held a number of advantages. They did not shake, rattle, roll, pollute, or make the noise of gasoline cars, such as Henry Ford's Model T. And while they had a limited driving range, they proved to be especially popular in cities, as well as with women drivers, because, without the need for a crank start, they were far easier to operate.

It may be startling to realize that at the beginning of the twentieth century, it was still an open question as to which form of power would prove to be the most popular in automobiles: 40 percent of automobiles at that time were powered by steam, 38 percent by electricity, and just 22 percent by gasoline. Sales of electric cars peaked in 1912, which was, not so coincidentally, the year before Henry Ford introduced the automated assembly line, making gasoline-powered cars affordable to nearly everyone. With that, the days of the electric car were numbered, and by the 1930s, the American electric automobile industry had effectively disappeared.

Today, of course, with high energy costs and the threat of global warming caused in part by emissions from fossil-fueled vehicles, there is a renewed interest in electric cars. Sales of hybrid vehicles, which run on both electricity and gasoline, have skyrocketed. And, in a promising development, in August 2009 General Motors announced that its new Chevrolet Volt would get an astounding city fuel economy of 230 miles per gallon (97.78 kilometers per liter). It will be interesting to see whether, in the years and decades to come, American automobile makers and consumers, so long enamored of the gasoline-powered engine, return to the days of old and the electric-powered car.

(continued from page 39)
with the piston once again at the top of the cylinder, the whole sequence is ready to begin again.

Otto sold his engine as a stationary motor, which could be attached to whatever the owner wanted to have powered. As with many other inventions, it would be up to somebody else to look at Otto's creation and imagine a new use for it.

It is a fact acknowledged by most historians that the first truly practical automobiles with internal combustion engines powered by gasoline were designed by several German inventors working at the same time. In 1885, in the city of Mannheim, Karl Benz built his first automobile and was granted a patent (DRP No. 37435) on January 29, 1886. It was a three-wheeler, and by 1888, Benz had begun manufacturing automobiles. Benz built his first four-wheel automobile in 1891, and by 1900 his company, Benz & Cie, became the world's largest manufacturer of automobiles. Today, his company, one of the pioneers in automobile manufacturing, is known as Mercedes-Benz.

At the same time, in 1889, Gottlieb Daimler and Wilhelm Maybach, working in Stuttgart, designed the first vehicle from scratch that was *meant* to be an automobile. Prior to that, the automobile had largely been a horse-drawn carriage simply refitted with an engine. (Daimler is also credited with building the prototype of the modern engine in 1885, improving on Otto's design. On March 8, 1886, Daimler attached his engine to a stagecoach, making what some believe to be the world's first four-wheeled automobile.)

THE BIRTH OF AN INDUSTRY

The idea of gasoline-powered automobiles took off, and by the early days of the twentieth century, they were outselling all other types of motor vehicles. But with their growing popularity came pressure on the manufacturers to increase production as quickly as possible.

Following Germany's Karl Benz, the world's first major car manufacturers were French. René Panhard and Émile Levassor built their first car in 1890, using a Daimler motor. But it was another French company, Peugeot, that illustrates the long road of discovery it took to get to the automobile.

The Peugeot family began their company in the 1700s, and by 1842, they had built themselves a nice business in the production of coffee, pepper, salt, and grinders. But that was not enough, and soon their company had expanded into bicycle manufacturing. Curiously enough, though, their entry into the vehicle market was made via women's clothing!

It seems that Peugeot was also in the business of making crinoline dresses, which used steel rods to expand the skirt outward from the woman's body. Manufacturing those steel rods led to umbrella frames, and then saw blades, wire wheels, and, ultimately bicycles. Armand Peugeot built his first bicycle, "Le Grand Bi," in 1882.

From there, it was an easy and logical progression to automobiles. Peugeot, after meeting with Gottlieb Daimler and others, decided that automobile production was where his company needed to go to survive. The first Peugeot automobile (a three-wheeled, steam-powered car) was built in 1889. In 1890, Peugeot built his first four-wheeled, gasoline-powered car. By 1903, of the world's total automobile production, nearly half, totaling 30,204 cars, were built in France.

In the United States, automobile production was just beginning to take off as well. Brothers Charles and Frank Duryea founded the Duryea Motor Company in 1893, becoming the first American automobile manufacturing company. Like Armand Peugeot, they were bicycle makers who became interested in gasoline engines and automobiles. The cars were by no means mass-produced (in 1896 the company sold just 13 copies of the model Duryea, an expensive limousine), but the company was involved in a very important first.

Peugeot, a company known for manufacturing grinders, bicycles, and crinoline skirts, created a four-wheel automobile after German engineers introduced the gas-powered engine to the world. By 1903, Peugeot was producing half the automobiles in the world.

In March 1896, the brothers offered for sale to the American public the first commercial automobile: the Duryea motor wagon. Just two months later, New York City driver Henry Wells hit a bicycle rider with his Duryea. The rider received a broken leg, Wells spent a night in jail, and the nation's first recorded traffic accident had occurred.

It would be up to another American, Ransom Eli Olds, to build the first mass-produced car in the United States. His interest in automobiles began when he was a young man, making steam and gasoline engines with his father, Pliny Fisk Olds, in Lansing, Michigan. He designed his first steam-powered car in 1887, and by 1899, with a growing experience and confidence in gasoline engines, moved to Detroit to start the Olds Motor Works. There, he began building what were at the time low-priced cars, making them on what was, in many ways, the first real assembly line.

Little is known about the details of Olds's assembly line, but the concept was enough that to many, he is considered to be the Father of the Assembly Line. Still, his company produced only 425 of his Curved Dash Olds in 1901 and increased production with the introduction of his assembly line in 1902 to just 2,500 vehicles. This increase in production, while honorable, was not nearly enough to meet the growing demand for automobiles. It was now time for Henry Ford to take the stage.

It would be Ford who would assemble the pieces of the puzzle that we have seen so far. It would be Ford who would add his own ideas and insights to what had been accomplished before him and introduce the world to the automated assembly line. But, who was Henry Ford?

Henry Ford

In his 1922 autobiography, *My Life and Work*, Henry Ford opens the chapter on his early life by indicating how his childhood shaped his later career:

> It was life on the farm that drove me into devising ways and means to better transportation. I was born on July 30, 1863, on a farm at Dearborn, Michigan, and my earliest recollection is that, considering the results, there was too much work on the place. That is the way I still feel about farming. There is a legend that my parents were very poor and that the early days were hard ones. Certainly they were not rich, but neither were they poor. As Michigan farmers went, we were prosperous. . . .
>
> There was too much hard hand labor on our own and all other farms of the time. Even when very young I suspected

that much might somehow be done in a better way. That is what took me into mechanics—although my mother always said I was born a mechanic. I had a kind of workshop with odds and ends of metal for tools before I had anything else. In those days, we did not have the toys of today; what we had were home made. My toys were all tools—they still are! And every fragment of machinery was a treasure.[1]

His father, William Ford, was an immigrant from County Cork, Ireland. His mother, Mary Litogot Ford, was born in Michigan, the child of Belgian immigrants. Henry Ford was the second child born to the Fords. Their first child, a boy born in 1862, died in infancy.

The genius of the assembly line was a lackluster student. According to historian Roger Burlingame, "He never learned to spell, to write a formed hand, to read freely, or to express himself in the simplest written sentence."[2] There was, however, one exception: "But from the earliest time of which there is a record he was a master of mechanical logic: from a glance at any machine he could understand interdependence of its parts—follow a line of reasoning, however long, through gears, ratchets, cams, and levels."[3]

It was, as we have seen, an age of new machines, of new technologies, of new means of transportation. And while William Ford tried to pass his love of nature and farming on to his son, Henry was not in the least bit interested. "He didn't like cows at all, and he didn't like horses,"[4] recalled his sister Margaret Ford Ruddiman. What he liked was working on machines, taking them apart and putting them back together again.

Fortunately for Henry, both his father and his mother encouraged his interest in tinkering and machines, but only up to a point. As Margaret remembered years later, "When we had mechanical or 'wind up' toys given to us at Christmas, we always said, 'Don't let Henry see them! He'll take them apart!'"[5] His mother did, however, go so far as to allow her oldest son to have a workbench in the kitchen. There, he could repair the toys of his younger brothers and sisters.

Although Henry did not do particularly well in school, there was one lesson he learned there that he carried with him throughout his life. The textbooks used in the one-room schoolhouse that Ford attended through eighth grade were the McGuffey Eclectic Reader series. These books taught the basics of reading, spelling, and grammar, as well as moral lessons for readers, one of which Ford took so much to heart that he memorized it: "Life will give you many unpleasant tasks to do: your duty will be hard and disagreeable and painful to you at times, but you must do it. You may have pity on others, but you must not pity yourself. Do what you find to do, and what you know you must do, to the best of your ability."[6]

The desire to do his duty, to work hard, did not apply to farm work, though. Nothing his father could say would be able to interest him in spending his life on the farm. The chances of that ever happening disappeared completely one day while Henry was traveling to Detroit with his father in the family buggy. Coming down the road toward them was a homemade portable steam engine, the first powered road vehicle he had ever seen.

It was not, as writer Douglas Brinkley pointed out, a particularly pretty sight. In Ford's own words, it was nothing more than a "boiler mounted on wheels with a water tank and a coal cart trailing behind it."[7] Despite its primitive appearance, it changed Ford's life. "I remember that engine as though I had seen it only yesterday," he wrote 50 years later. It was at that moment that Ford reached the decision: his life would be dedicated to building "machines that moved."[8]

CHASING HIS DREAM

Ford quit school in 1879 and left home to find work as an apprentice machinist in Detroit. Living with his aunt, he found immediate work building streetcars at the Michigan

Henry Ford grew up on a farm in Michigan, but he had no interest in agriculture; he was focused on machines. After completing two apprenticeships that involved heavy machinery, Ford moved to Detroit so he could learn about electricity with the Edison Illuminating Company.

Car Company Works. Unfortunately, he was fired after only six days for reasons that have never been determined.

With his father's help, he was given an apprenticeship at the James Flower & Brothers Machine Shop, which designed and manufactured brass and iron machine parts. For a 60-hour work week, Ford earned just $2.50—one dollar less than his aunt was charging him for room and board. So 16-year-old Henry was forced to supplement his meager earnings by working nights repairing clocks and watches for a local jeweler.

After finishing his apprenticeship with James Flower, he took another one at Detroit Dry Dock. This job paid even less than the one he had had before—only $2 a week—and Ford soon realized that he could not afford to remain in Detroit. In the spring of 1882, nearly 20 years old, he returned home to Dearborn. There, his father hoped that Henry had finally gotten the idea of working on machines in the big city out of his system and was ready to settle down and take over the business of the family farm.

It was not to be. Living next door to the Fords was John Gleason, a fellow farmer who had just purchased a new Westinghouse steam engine. His plan was to rent it out to local farmers, who could use it to power their own equipment. There was one small problem, though. Gleason's employees, as well as the local farmers, were afraid of the new engine and did not know how to operate it. Henry Ford did.

It was, he fondly recalled years later, the best job he ever had. "I was paid three dollars a day and had 83 days of steady work. I traveled from farm to farm and I threshed our own and our neighbor's clover, hauled loads, cut corn stalks, ground feed, sawed wood. It was hard work."[9]

All that hard work paid big dividends. The first summer he spent operating the engine, he met an agent of the Westinghouse Company. He was hired on the spot to be the company's full-time demonstrator and repairman. This meant that whenever a piece of Westinghouse equipment broke down anywhere in southern Michigan, it was Ford who was sent to repair it.

Now, although he was still living on his father's farm, he was not doing any farming. He repaired steam engines; he tinkered in his own workshop and took night classes in accounting, typing, mechanical drawing, and general business at downtown Detroit's Goldsmith, Bryant and Stratton Business College. It was there, at the age of 21, that he met 18-year-old Clara Jane Bryant.

The couple married on April 11, 1888, settling into life as newlyweds on a farm adjoining the Fords'. But soon enough, Henry Ford was restless. He knew he did not want to live on a farm all his life. He knew he wanted more, far more than that. He began making plans to return to Detroit, certain that he could find work there, hopefully with the Edison Illuminating Company.

When Ford worked at the Detroit Dry Dock, he had seen an Otto four-stroke motor. He had read about the first automobiles being built in Europe. He began to put the pieces together, realizing that maybe he could find a way to build automobiles in America, using a motor similar to the Otto. The difference would be that this one would be much more affordable and practical than the ones being built in Europe.

But there was one snag. The four-stroke engine was fired by the explosion of electricity coming from the spark plug, and while Ford knew almost everything there was to know about the rest of the engine, he still did not know a lot about electricity. By working at the Edison Illuminating Company, Thomas Edison's own electric company in Detroit, Ford would be able to fill in the missing parts of his mechanical education.

With his background in engine repair, Ford was offered the job of night engineer, working from 6:00 P.M. to 6:00 A.M. Soon enough, he learned what he needed to know and quickly became an expert at keeping the plant's generator operating all by himself. He was soon promoted to chief engineer, making the relatively princely wage of $1,000 a year.

Somehow, despite being on call 24 hours a day, seven days a week, Ford still found time to tinker in his home workshop. On Christmas Eve of 1893, Ford tested his own home-built gasoline engine. It had only one cylinder and was crafted out of a piece of metal pipe he had brought home from the plant, along with other scrap materials. He ran a wire from the engine to an overhead light socket for the electrical current he needed. After just one failed sputtering attempt, the engine worked.

Ford was now more determined than ever to build his own automobile. And, despite his continued success at Edison, he knew that it was not the career he wanted. So he began to recruit fellow dreamers and engineers to help him achieve his own dream. One fellow Edison employee went to work to design the ignition system. A friend helped supply parts, while yet another friend helped to build the vehicle in a shed behind the Fords' duplex.

It took three long years to build. Much to Ford's dismay, while he was still building his car, another Detroiter, Charles King, drove his own hand-built car down St. Antoine Street. Although basically nothing more than a wooden wagon driven by a four-cylinder engine, it was still the first "automobile" seen in Detroit.

Obviously, Ford was disappointed that his was not the first automobile in Detroit. But he received encouragement in his dream from a very important source—Thomas Edison himself. Ford was introduced to the great man at a convention in New York. Edison was already aware of Ford and his desire to build automobiles.

Seizing the opportunity, Ford quickly explained to Edison what he meant to do. Edison immediately grasped the possibilities and urged Ford to continue in his quest. "Young man, that's the thing! Your car is self-contained, no boiler, no heavy battery, no smoke or steam. Keep at it!"[10] That was all Ford needed to hear. Three months later, he was ready to test his first car, which he called the Quadricycle.

In his free time away from the Edison Illuminating Company, Ford tinkered away in his workshop. Located in a shed in his backyard, Ford's workshop was where he would put together his first automobile, known as the Quadricycle.

It was an ungainly contraption, nothing more than the frame from an old horse buggy placed on top of four bicycle wheels. The four-horsepower gasoline engine was mounted behind the seat. The simple transmission was a rubber belt leading from the engine to the rear wheels. There was no brake. There was no reverse gear.

It was four o'clock in the morning of June 4, 1896, when Ford showed the Quadricycle to his wife, Clara, and his friend Jim Bishop. As he got into the car to take it for its test drive, he realized he had a serious problem. The car had been assembled in the shed piece by piece. It was only now when it was completed that he realized, much to his embarrassment, that the car would not fit through the door of the shed!

The solution was simple. Ford just grabbed an ax and chopped a hole in the shed's brick wall large enough to wheel his car through. In his book *Wheels for the World*, Douglas Brinkley described the historic moment when Henry Ford drove his first motorized vehicle onto the streets of Detroit:

> The proud machinist opened the current from his battery and adjusted the fuel intake by pinching the valve between his thumb and forefinger to serve as a choke. Next, Ford reached into the engine compartment and jerked the flywheel to start it spinning, and as soon as the motor started he clambered up onto the driver's seat. He pulled back the lever to tighten the belt that ran around the rear axle, grasped the tiller, and an instant later a machine built of his own ambition was carrying Henry Ford forward, down Grand River Avenue. With Jim Bishop bicycling ahead to warn off the few carriages and pedestrians on the streets at that hour, Ford made a circle around three main thoroughfares. Only one breakdown on Washington Boulevard marred the trip, caused by a faulty spring that required Ford and Bishop to push the quadricycle over to the Edison plant to fetch a new one.[11]

Henry Ford sold his Quadricycle for $200. It was the first car he ever sold. It would not be the last.

FIRST VENTURES

Although Ford dreamed of building automobiles, he was now 36 years old, with a wife and a son to support. He had a good, paying position with Edison, and in 1899 he was offered a promotion to plant superintendent. While the job would have meant an increase in pay, the added responsibilities would have made it impossible for him to continue auto building.

"I had to choose between my job and the automobile,"[12] Ford said later. The answer, however, was never in doubt. With financial banking from Detroit lumber baron William H. Murphy, Ford resigned from Edison and founded the Detroit Automobile Company on August 5, 1899.

The company was a failure. Ford was still feeling his way, trying to figure out the best, most price-effective way to build automobiles. Over a 15-month period, only 12 trucks were built, and they ended up being sold for scrap. In need of money, Ford turned to a relatively new and novel use for cars: racing.

With the assistance of his associate C. Harold Wills, Ford designed, built, and then successfully raced a 26-horsepower automobile against veteran racer Alexander Winston. Winton's car was more powerful than Ford's, and Winston had won more automobile races than any other man alive. Still, Ford managed to win, but how? The engine on Winston's car broke down, allowing Ford's better-built car to pull ahead for the victory.

While his only reward for the victory was a crystal bowl, he also earned a great deal of favorable publicity. A new group of investors, including some from the failed Detroit Automobile Company, formed the Henry Ford Company on November 30, 1901, hiring Ford as the company's chief engineer. But Ford had disagreements with other investors and left the company in 1902 with just $900 and the rights to his name. With his departure, the company was renamed the Cadillac Automobile Company, which quickly established itself as one of America's premier builders of luxury cars.

Once again, Ford turned to auto racing, designing the 999, which had an 80-horsepower engine. He hired famous bicycle racer Barney Oldfield to race in it against Alexander Winston, whom he easily defeated. (The next year, Oldfield became the first man to drive a car around an oval at the then unprecedented speed of 60 miles per hour, or 96.6 kph.) Ford enjoyed

(continues on page 58)

THE ANTI-SEMITISM OF HENRY FORD

Henry Ford may be an American hero, but he was a human being, with flaws like just like anyone. One of his biggest flaws was his anti-Semitism, an intense distrust and hatred of people who are Jewish.

As one of America's richest and most powerful men, Ford was, unfortunately, in a position to share his views with the nation and the world. Using his own newspaper, the *Dearborn Independent*, as his mouthpiece, Ford published a series of attacks on Jews during the years 1920 to 1927. Among them was a reprint of the notorious *Protocols of the Learned Elders of Zion*, a forged document possibly written by Russian aristocrats, which alleged an evil and sinister Jewish plot to take over the world. The newspaper also falsely claimed that Christopher Columbus's voyage to America in 1492 had been part of a Jewish plot to conquer the New World. The newspaper even claimed, falsely, that it had been Jews who were behind the assassination of Abraham Lincoln.

All of this would have been bad enough, but in the early 1920s, a four-volume set of the newspaper's articles, collectively titled *The International Jew: The World's Foremost Problem*, was published both in the United States and in Europe. In chapters with titles such as "How Jews in the U.S. Conceal Their Strength," "The High and Low of Jewish Money Power," "Jewish Gamblers Corrupt American Baseball," and "Angles of Jewish Influence in American Life," the book draws a startling and yet totally untrue picture of the power and influence of Jews to control and corrupt every aspect of American (as well as world) life. As Ford wrote, "When there is something wrong in this country, you'll find the Jews."*

Unfortunately, the book, which condoned the use of violence against Jews, found an avid audience in Germany and in its fastest-growing political party, the National Socialist German Workers' Party, better known to history as the Nazis.

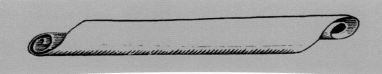

The head of the party, Adolf Hitler, who within the next 10 years would become Germany's chancellor and lead the world into World War II, read and admired Ford's publications. Indeed, Ford is the only American Hitler wrote about in his own book, *Mein Kampf*, calling him his greatest inspiration.

In 1923, Hitler bemoaned the fact that he could not assist with the ultimately unsuccessful "Henry Ford for President" movement, telling a reporter for the *Chicago Tribune* that "I wish I could send some of my shock troops to Chicago and other big American cities to help in the elections. . . . We look to Heinrich Ford as the leader of the growing Fascist movement in America."** Ultimately, in July 1938, Hitler awarded Ford the Grand Cross of the German Eagle, the highest medal awarded by Nazi Germany to foreigners.

In the United Sates, although readership for the *Dearborn Independent* ran as high as 700,000 people, Ford was strongly criticized for his beliefs. The Anti-Defamation League condemned him, as did former U.S. president and chief justice of the Supreme Court William Howard Taft. Speaking in December 1920 in Chicago, Taft said: "One of the chief causes of suffering and evil in the world today is race hatred, and any man who stimulates that hatred has much to answer for. When he does this by the circulation of unfounded and the arousing of mean and groundless fears, his fault is more to be condemned."*** Although in later years Ford's views on Jews moderated to some extent, the damage had already been done. His anti-Semitism remains a stain on his life that can never be erased.

* John Bankston, *Henry Ford and the Assembly Line*. Bear, Del.: Mitchell Lane Publishers, 2004, p. 43.
** Douglas Brinkley, *Wheels for the World: Henry Ford, His Company, and a Century of Progress, 1903–2003*. New York: Penguin Books, 2003, p. 263.
*** Ibid.

(continued from page 55)
auto racing (he himself drove his car at the then world record pace of 91 miles per hour, or 146.5 kph), but it was not enough to satisfy him.

With the backing of Alexander Y. Malcomson, the partnership Ford & Malcomson Ltd. was formed to manufacture automobiles. Ford had been hard at work designing an inexpensive automobile, and the partners leased a factory and contracted with a machine shop owned by John and Horace E. Dodge to supply more than $166,000 in parts.

Sales were slow, and the Dodge brothers soon demanded payment for their parts. Once again, a new group of investors had to be brought in, and the Dodge brothers were convinced to accept a part of the new company as payment. On June 16, 1903, Ford & Malcomson was reborn as the Ford Motor Company. Just five years later, history would be made when the first Model T Ford was built.

The Birth of
the Automated
Assembly Line

The Ford Motor Company was named in honor of Henry Ford, the man who many considered to know more about automobiles than anyone in the country. Yet the company was not his to control. He was the company's chief engineer, but the real power lay with Alexander Y. Malcomson, who was financing the operation, and his clerk James Couzens. It would be up to Couzens, who believed in Ford's dream of building an automobile for the masses, to help keep Ford focused on the task at hand. The first car produced by the Ford Motor Company was, naturally enough, the Model A. (The first car was sold to Dr. Ernest Pfenning of Chicago, Illinois, on July 23, 1903.) Between 1903 and 1904, 1,708 Model A Fords left the company's Mack Avenue plant. Priced at $850 ($20,905 today), the car, while less than the average worker's yearly wage, was still out of the range of most.

The car was popular, and the Ford Motor Company began to make a profit. But Ford was already eager to press on and find a way to speed up the process of assembly to help lower the cost of his car. Malcomson, on the other hand, wanted to push the company in another direction. He wanted to build more expensive cars that, while not selling in large numbers, would appeal to those who wanted to buy a luxury car.

For a time, it looked like Malcomson would win out. The next car built by Ford, the Model B, was a luxury motorcar that sold for $2,000 (nearly $50,000 today), more than twice the price of the Model A. The car also sold well, allowing Ford to move operations from Mack Avenue to a space 10 times larger, on Detroit's Piquette Avenue. Along the top of the building stood a large sign, proclaiming proudly, "The Home of the Celebrated Ford Automobile."[1]

By 1905, 25 Fords a day were being manufactured at Piquette Avenue, assembled by a workforce of almost 300. New models followed the B: the Models C, E, F, K, N, R, and S. The company was doing well, but Ford was not satisfied. He still was not building the car that he wanted to build. He was not building cars the way he wanted to build them, the way he knew they could be built—quickly, using an automated system.

Ford realized that there was a huge untapped market for an inexpensive car. By 1906, he was saying, "The greatest need today is a light, low-priced car with an up-to-date engine of ample horsepower, built of the very best material . . . it must be powerful enough for American roads and capable of carrying its passengers anywhere that a horse-drawn vehicle will go without the driver being afraid of ruining his car."[2]

But that car would never be built as long as Malcomson was with Ford. In an effort to sidestep him, Ford and Couzens set up the Ford Manufacturing Company, a separate entity whose function was to build the parts that would be used in Ford Motor Company cars. It was the first time that Ford began manufacturing all of the parts used in his vehicles. But

Ford wanted to manufacture inexpensive cars that could be driven over any terrain, and he deftly wrested control of the Ford Motor Company to direct it away from producing luxury automobiles.

the company also served a second purpose—Malcomson was given no part of the new company. Outmaneuvered, he sold his shares of the Ford Motor Company in 1906.

The stock was purchased by Ford and Couzens. After a brief power struggle with the company's board of directors, Henry Ford was elected president of Ford Motor in July 1907. The company that bore his name was now his to operate, along with James Couzens, in any way he wanted. It was time for Ford to begin building the car he had long dreamed of.

BUILDING THE MODEL T

Ford employee Charles Sorenson remembered the day Henry Ford summoned him in the Piquette Avenue plant: "I followed him to the third floor and its north end, which was not fully occupied for assembly work. He looked about and said, 'Charlie, I'd like to have a room finished off right here in this space. Put up a wall with a door in big enough to run a car in and out. . . . We're going to start a completely new job.'"[3]

That room at the Piquette Street plant became the birthplace of the Model T Ford. Sorenson wrote that the room was soon built and equipped with power tools and blackboards. "The blackboards . . . gave a king-sized drawing which, when all initial refinements had been made, could be photographed for two purposes; as a protection against patent suits attempting to prove prior claim to originality and as a substitute for blueprints. A little more than a year later, Model T, the product of that cluttered room was announced to the world."[4]

It would prove to be the car that changed everything. Equipped with a four-cylinder engine that was started by turning a crank, with two forward speeds and a reverse, run by foot pedals, the first car built with the steering wheel on the left, and with a clunky-looking frame built high off the ground to allow it to drive in the roughest of conditions, it would never win a beauty contest. But it was what Ford always wanted—a safe, reliable car that was easy to repair.

Years earlier, *Nation* magazine had predicted that "as soon as a standard cheap car can be produced, of a simple type that does not require mechanical aptitude in the operator, and that may be run inexpensively, there will be no limit to the automobile market."[5] The Model T would prove them correct.

As Henry Ford proudly proclaimed when introducing his dream for the Model T:

> I will build a motor car for the great multitude . . . it will be so low in price that no man making a good salary

will be unable to own one and enjoy with his family the blessing of hours in God's great open spaces. . . . When I'm through, everybody will be able to afford one, and

THE COLOR OF THE MODEL T

During the first few years of production, while the Model T was still being built without the benefit of the automated assembly line, the car was available to consumers in a variety of colors: red for touring cars and gray for roadsters, with black and green also available. But by 1911, it became clear to Ford that he could sell as many cars as he could manufacture no matter what color they were, so, to further simplify and streamline the manufacturing process, he decided to produce the Model T in just one color, a dark Brewster green, with red striping.

There were still problems, however. The cars required 14 coats of paint to get a quality finish. Each of those 14 coats had to dry thoroughly before the next coat could be applied. Depending on the humidity, it could take an entire day for one single coat to dry, after which it would then have to be sanded by hand before the next coat could be added. Taking up to two weeks to paint one car was, clearly, unacceptable to Ford and his team of engineers. Something would have to change.

The solution proved to be simple. As it turned out, black paint dried much more quickly than colored paint. To completely finish a body in black took no more than a day and a half, as opposed to the two weeks necessary to produce cars in any other color. Given that, it should come as no surprise that by 1914, all Model Ts, without exception, were sold to the consumer in black. As Henry Ford was often credited as saying, "You can have a Model T in any color you want, as long as it's black."

everyone will have one. The horse will have disappeared from our highways, the automobile will be taken for granted . . . and we will give a large number of men employment at good wages.[6]

When it was introduced in 1908, the car was manufactured using the techniques that Ford had been using. The assembly was still done by hand, although the parts were machine made and interchangeable. Indeed, as plant supervisor Max Wollering said: "One of Mr. Ford's strong points was the interchangeability of parts. He realized as well as any other manufacturer realized that in order to create quantity of production, your interchangeability must be fine and unique in order to accomplish the rapid assembly of units. There can't be much hand work or fitting if you are going to accomplish great things."[7]

To help sell his car, Ford mounted a massive advertising campaign to inform the public that the car it had long been waiting for was now available. (The car, originally priced at $825—around $20,290 today—was within the price range of a large number of consumers. Little did those early buyers know, though, that with the introduction of the assembly line, within eight years the price would drop by more than half.)

But even at $825, production was unable to keep up with demand. Only 11 cars were built at the Piquette plant during the first full month of production. More and more machines were being used in the manufacturing process, but it was not enough. To be able to produce the Model T in the numbers that were demanded by the public, Ford would have to build his "Tin Lizzie" in an entirely new way.

HIGHLAND PARK

Back in 1906, Ford had purchased 60 acres (24.28 hectares) of land at Highland Park on the north side of Detroit and set to work to build the most modern factory imaginable. For perhaps the first time, a factory was being built and designed with the sole purpose of manufacturing a product in the most efficient manner possible.

Ford made the decision to stop work on all other models and focus exclusively on the Model T. Machines were designed and built; every part was machined and checked. Engineers were brought in to arrange the machines in the most logical and efficient way possible. A work-scheduling system was devised to record the output that each machine could achieve in a day.

Special attention was paid to interchangeability of parts—to make certain that each part was absolutely identical to another. Accuracy was the top goal. For example, the Ford team built milling machine fixtures and tables that could hold 15 engine blocks at a time. Each one was easily snapped into place and held rigidly with similar devices built to hold 30 cylinder heads at once. Witnesses marveled at the fact that the two pieces, the head and the block, could be brought together with only a plain gasket—no longer was there the need for time-consuming, labor-intensive joint scraping just to make the parts fit.

By 1913, it was no secret that Ford machinery was the best in the world. In addition, because Ford had made the decision to manufacture *only* the Model T, his engineers had the opportunity to install single-purpose machine tools. Focusing on manufacturing just *one* kind of part for just *one* kind of automobile simplified matters and allowed Ford's engineers to create whole new systems of doing things. By the time they were done, there were no fitters in any Ford assembly department. Interchangeability had been achieved.

The next step would be the biggest. Now that the parts were there, what would be the fastest and most efficient way to put them all together? Several years earlier, Ford had visited a slaughterhouse and had seen animal carcasses hanging from moving conveyor belts, past workers who would each cut or remove a specific part of the animal. It was, in effect, a disassembly line. Maybe the process could be worked in reverse?

The idea was a simple one. Instead of men moving to the work, why not move the work to the men? The idea is such a basic one, and its development at the Highland Park factory came so quickly, that it is impossible to give any single person credit for its development. Ultimately, though, it was Henry Ford who brought the best and brightest people together and set them to work to create a system that would allow him to build his Model T at a rate never before achieved.

The first assembly line started on April 1, 1913, in the Ford flywheel magneto assembling department. Previously, the workers had each had their own individual workbench, where they would put together the many parts necessary to build a flywheel. On that day, though, things would be done differently.

Each of the workers stood beside a long, waist-high row of flywheels. The workers had been instructed by their foreman to "place one particular part in the assembly or perhaps start a few nuts or even just tighten them and then push the flywheel down the row to the next worker. Having pushed it down eighteen or perhaps thirty-six inches, the workers repeated the same process, over and over, nine hours, over and over,"[8] according to David A. Hounshell.

It was a major breakthrough. Twenty-nine workers, who had each assembled between 35 and 40 flywheels on their own, put together a total of 1,118 of them on the line. Building the flywheels individually had taken approximately 20 minutes each; on the line it took only 13 minutes and 10 seconds. But although it was a good start, the system was not quite there yet.

Some workers complained about back problems because the line was too low, so it was raised an additional 6 inches (15.24 cm). The other problem was more fundamental: Some workers moved too slowly, while others moved too fast. Here was where the last major breakthrough in the assembly line process occurred. What if, instead of having each worker finish

Ford's first modern assembly line was designed to build flywheels, an important part of the Model T. Workers lined up alongside a bench repeated the same task over and over again as the equipment moved from person to person.

a piece and move it on, the pieces were moved at a set rate by means of a chain?

By doing so, the foreman would be able to set the pace for all of his workers. The slow ones would be forced to work faster, while the fast ones would be forced to slow down and do quality work. Within just one year, by raising the height of the line, moving the flywheels with the use of a continuous chain, and cutting the number of workers down to 14, 1,335 flywheels were being assembled each eight-hour day. What once took 20 minutes to assemble now took just 5. The automated assembly line was born.

As David E. Nye pointed out in his book *Consuming Powers: A Social History of American Energies*, the time was right for the automated assembly line to come into being. It was the combination of five practices, "subdivision of labor, interchangeable parts, single-function machines, sequential ordering of machines, and the moving belt,"[9] that defined the assembly line. All of them were in existence, but with the increase in factory electrification, it was now possible to use electricity to power the engines needed to power the assembly line.

Within months, assembly lines were in place to put together each of the parts that went into building the Model T. In August 1913, the first attempt was made to assemble the car itself along an assembly line. Ropes were used to pull the car's chassis past the various parts that would go into the completed car. What once took 12.5 man-hours to build was cut to just 5.83 man-hours.

Experiments continued, some of which worked while others did not, as Ford engineers worked to put together the final pieces of the puzzle. What was the best speed to move the line? Where should the workers be standing? How many or how few workers were needed? What was the best way to get the parts to the workers?

By the end of April 1914, three lines were running full swing, with workers putting together 1,212 chassis assemblies in eight hours—just 93 man-minutes per vehicle. On June 1, 1914, a chain-driven assembly line was put in use for front axle assemblies. This reduced the assembly time from 150 minutes to just 26.5 minutes. Throughout the Ford Motor Company, automated assembly lines were in place, allowing parts and entire automobiles to be put together at a truly astonishing pace.

The figures tell the story. In 1912, a total of 82,388 Model T cars were produced. Just three years later, in 1915, a total of

230,788 Model Ts were produced. In 1912, it took a total of 1,260 man-hours to assemble one Model T Ford. Two years later, that number had been cut to 617. By 1923, a Model T Ford could be built from start to finish in only 228 man-hours.

For the first time in human history, the automated assembly line was being used to manufacture products faster than ever thought possible. It was the beginning of a new world of manufacturing. David E. Nye explained that not only did the assembly line allow management to control the speed with which work was done, it also allowed management to closely monitor the workers' individual performance.

Gone were the workshops of highly trained workers and artisans. In its place was something entirely new and different, as described by Englishman Julian Street in his book, *Abroad at Home*:

> To my mind, unaccustomed to such things, the whole room, with its interminable aisles, its whirling shafts and wheels, its forest of roof-supporting posts and flapping, flying, leather belting, its endless rows of writhing machinery; its shrieking, hammering, and clatter, its smell of oil, its autumn haze of smoke, its savage-looking foreign population—to my mind it expressed but one thing and that was delirium. . . .
>
> Fancy a jungle of wheels and belts and weird iron forms— of men, machinery and movement—add to it every kind of sound you can imagine; the sound of a million squirrels chirking, a million monkeys quarreling, a million lions roaring, a million pigs dying, a million elephants smashing through a forest of sheet iron, a million boys whistling on their fingers, a million others coughing with the whooping cough, a million sinners groaning as they are being dragged to hell—imagine all of this happening at the very edge of Niagara Falls, with the everlasting roar of the cataract as a perpetual background, and you may acquire a vague conception of that place.[10]

It was the dawn of a new era. Years later, Henry Ford was involved in a heated discussion about education with a young man who grew angered at what he saw as Ford's conservative views. "These are different times: this is the modern age," he told Ford. "Young man," Ford snapped back, "I invented the modern age."[11]

Unexpected Consequences

The automated assembly line was first seen at the Ford Motor Company in 1913. But Henry Ford did not try to keep the idea to himself. He allowed both journalists and other manufacturers to tour his plant, eager to show them the "secret" of his success. Soon enough, assembly lines began popping up in factories all across the United States. Production levels of products of all kinds skyrocketed, and the country soon began to see an abundance never before seen.

Manufacturers were happy because they were producing more products at a lower cost. Consumers were happy because, due to lower production costs, the price to purchase manufactured items was dropping faster than they ever imagined possible. For example, the same Model T Ford that had cost $850 in 1908 was selling for just $490 in 1914 and the remarkable price of $260 in 1924. With prices that low, it has been said that by the 1920s, a majority of American drivers had learned to drive on a Model T.

The only people who were not happy about the automated assembly line were the workers themselves. Their work was now highly regimented and, because they were performing the same simple tasks over and over again, highly monotonous. Trained workers who were once considered craftspeople were now just parts of a larger machine, a machine designed to build cars as quickly as possible.

Those one-time craftspeople were soon replaced by low-priced, unskilled workers. Large numbers of immigrants from eastern, central, and southern Europe had been flooding the United States in search of jobs. These workers, with little education and little understanding of the English language, could easily be trained to perform a simple task, such as tightening nut number 86 over and over and over again. Indeed, by 1914, 71 percent of all Ford workers were foreign-born.

No thinking was necessary in the new world of the assembly line. The only responsibility the workers had was to keep pace with the machines. This often became a test of their patience and determination. As an unidentified Ford worker once said, "If I have to put on nut #86 86 more times I will be nut #86 in the bunk house."[1] To boost productivity, the line foreman would often turn up the speed on the line just a bit, forcing workers to go faster.

But he would not stop there. He would turn it up another notch, and then another notch, until the workers were moving as fast as humanly possible. The foreman would then turn it back down one notch, just enough to keep the workers from going mad. But in the meantime, he would get an extra 10 to 15 machines built in the process.

Henry Ford seemed to believe that most people enjoyed doing repetitive work. "Most people," however, did not seem to include himself. "Repetitive labor—the doing of one thing over and over again and always the same way—is a terrifying

When a wave of immigrants arrived in the United States, factories that had adopted Ford's manufacturing techniques were able to hire these new Americans and train them to work on an assembly line. Because this was more cost-effective and more efficient than using individual crafts-men, companies were able to produce more of their products at a lower cost to the consumer.

prospect to a certain kind of mind. It is terrifying to me. I could not possibly do the same thing day in and day out. But, to other minds, perhaps I might say to the majority of minds, repetitive operations hold no terrors. In fact, to some types of minds, thought is absolutely appalling."[2]

Not surprisingly, despite Ford's belief in the dislike that many had for thinking, workers folded under the pressure of working on the line. By the end of 1913, the Ford Motor Company was seeing a 380 percent turnover rate in its employees. Absenteeism had become so frequent and prevalent that it became known as "Forditis." Historian Keith Sward wrote, "So great was labor's distaste for the new machine system that toward the close of 1913 every time the company wanted to add 100 men to its personnel, it was necessary to hire 963."[3]

Workers, it seemed, were not content to be paid low wages—as low as just 25 cents per hour working a 10-hour day—just to be seen as parts of a machine, as interchangeable as the parts they themselves were building.

It was an impossible situation for the Ford Motor Company. Under the system that Henry Ford had put in place, every part manufactured there followed a predetermined path, going place by place through the plant. If a person was missing from one place, the whole system came to a screeching halt.

So, if at any one time 14,000 workers were needed to keep the plant going, and 10 percent of those were absent at any given time (the average number), that meant that an additional 1,400 workers were required each and every day just to fill in the gaps. It was obvious that something had to change so that workers could be inspired to do work they hated. The solution, although radical at the time, was obvious.

THE FIVE-DOLLAR DAY

It is important to understand the tumultuous relationship between labor and management occurring at that time. In

1914, the Commission on Industrial Relations reported that 35,000 workers had been killed and another 700,000 injured in industrial accidents in the previous year. Job-related diseases were common, and hourly wages, even for skilled workers, were as low as 15 cents an hour.

To most workers, it seemed that management cared nothing about its employees. Strikes, picketing, and a call for unions were becoming more and more common. And, as Douglas Brinkley pointed out in his book *Wheels for the World*, many millionaire tycoons seemed to have nothing but contempt for the "rabble" who were working for them and making them rich.

Glenn Porter, writing of one such tycoon in *The Worker's World at Hagley*, said, "He always had a large bag of dimes and nickels and he threw them up in the air and watched us scramble for them."[4] Jack London, the American writer best known for his novel *The Call of the Wild* and his short story "To Build a Fire," described the tension between workers and management in his 1907 novel *The Iron Heel*. "In the face of the facts that modern man lives more wretchedly than the cave-man, no other conclusion is possible than that the capitalist class has mismanaged . . . criminally and selfishly mismanaged."[5]

But with one stroke, Henry Ford changed all that and helped bring about a new relationship between labor and management. On January 5, 1914, the Ford Motor Company held a press conference to make an announcement. Only three reporters were present to hear James Couzens, by that time the vice president, treasurer, and public spokesperson for Ford, read the following statement:

> The Ford Motor Company, the greatest and most successful automobile manufacturing company in the world will, on January 12, inaugurate the greatest revolution in the matter of rewards for its workers ever known to the industrial world.
>
> At one stroke it will reduce the hours of labor from nine to eight, and add to every man's pay a share of the profits of

the house. The smallest to be received by a man 22 years old and upwards will be $5 per day.[6]

It was an announcement heard throughout the country. Ford workers were ecstatic. "In January 1914," recalled Logan Miller, "it was announced that Ford was going to pay a mini-

FORDLANDIA

By 1928, the Ford Motor Company was manufacturing so many automobiles and trucks that Henry Ford decided that the company needed its own source of rubber for the tires for those vehicles. To do so, Ford negotiated with the government of Brazil to grant him approximately 2.5 million acres (10,000 sq. km) of land located on the banks of the Rio Tapajos, near the city of Santarém, Brazil. In exchange, the government would receive a 9 percent interest in the company's profits.

It would, however, be more than just another rubber plantation. Ford's dream was to build an American midwestern town in the jungles of the Amazon, complete with plumbing, hospitals, schools, sidewalks, tennis courts, and even a golf course. Residents and workers at Fordlandia would have to live by a strict set of rules: There would be no alcohol, tobacco, or other forms of what Ford considered immoral behavior. Each resident would be required to build a garden, and dances would be held each week.

The idea, as author Greg Grandin said in his recent book *Fordlandia: The Rise and Fall of Henry Ford's Forgotten Jungle City*, was to do more than extract raw materials from the Amazon jungle. Fordlandia would be "an example of his particular dream, of how Ford-style capitalism—high wages, humane benefits and moral improvement—could bring prosperity to a benighted land."*

Unfortunately, the workers, both the imported Americans and the native Brazilians, did not enjoy working under Ford's strict rules.

mum wage of $5 a day. At that time I was getting $0.32 an hour."[7] Miller, and thousands of other workers like him, had seen their wages doubled to 62.5 cents per hour.

(It is important to look at those wages in context. At that time, steelworkers were making an average of $1.75 per day. Coal miners were making around $2.50. In 1911, a government

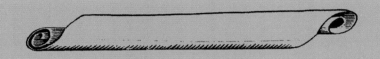

Since workers could not drink on company property, they went off property to drink and carouse in the bars and bordellos that quickly set up business nearby. Diseases such as malaria, yellow fever, and other tropical illnesses sickened or killed many residents. When cafeteria service was introduced in the company dining rooms to take the place of waiter service, a riot broke out, with the men destroying the mess hall and every vehicle on the property.

Fordlandia might have survived those problems, but there was one problem Ford could not get around. None of Ford's managers (imported from America) had the knowledge required to successfully manage a rubber plantation. As Grandin said, "What [Fordlandia] didn't have was a horticulturist, agronomist, microbiologist, entomologist, or any other person who might know something about jungle rubber and its enemies."** Ford's rubber trees fell victim to bugs, leaf blight, and swarms of caterpillars that stripped the trees bare.

It was a losing battle. In 1945, Ford sold Fordlandia back to the Brazilian government for $244,200. The remains of Fordlandia still stand in the Amazon jungle—a monument to Henry Ford's failed dream.

---

* Ben MacIntyre, "Dearborn-on-Amazon," a review of *Fordlandia: The Rise and Fall of Henry Ford's Forgotten Jungle City, New York Times,* July 16, 2009. http://www.nytimes.com/2009/07/19/books/review/Macintyre-t.html.
** Ibid.

survey concluded that over half of all male workers earned less than $600 per year, even though $800 a year was considered the minimum income necessary for a man to support the average family of a wife and three children. Ford's $5 a day gave workers earnings of $1,200 a year.)

While Ford's workers were thrilled at the news, newspapers and other business owners were outraged. George Brown, who was working at Ford Motor at the time, recalled: "When Mr. Ford announced that he was going to pay the laboring man in the plant $5 a day, why, he just upset the whole financial situation. As I remember, the newspapers came out and just as much as said that Henry Ford was due for an insane asylum. Why, it was something unheard of to pay a man $5 a day from $2.34. It was just double the figure. They thought he was crazy."[8]

Of course, technically, it was not exactly an increase in salary. As the announcement said, pay was going to be increased based on the company's profits. The idea was that those profits would be paid in advance to the workers. If the company did well in 1914, everybody would share in its success. If the company did not do well, in the following year, wages would drop back to their original level. But of course, once workers got a taste of higher wages, they were more than willing to work hard to insure that they stayed there.

Productivity skyrocketed. Douglas Brinkley gives the example of one worker who doubled his output of parts for a subassembly. When production chief Bill Knudsen asked him how he managed to do so, the man replied in halting English: "Mr. Ford pay me two-fifty, he get 250 pieces. Mr. Ford now pay me five dollars a day, he get 500 pieces. I pay him back."[9] It seemed that workers were more than willing to trade higher wages for rotten working conditions.

Not only did it turn out that workers were willing to work harder for higher wages, it also turned out that people were willing to turn out in droves just for the opportunity to apply for the new high-paying jobs. Worker George Brown remembered the events of the day following the announcement of the $5-a-day wage: "The next day it was a sight there on Manchester Avenue. That place was packed so that a human being couldn't move! Everybody wanted to work at Ford Motor then at $5 a day, because that was better than doubling a man's wage."[10]

Indeed, the promise of $5 a day led 10,000 men to make their way up Woodward Avenue that day in freezing winter weather in search of work. One week later, on January 12, 12,000 people waited outside the company gates in search of work. The crowds grew so restless that the Highland Fire Department was called in to disperse the crowd by turning water hoses on them in icy weather.

It was not only residents of Detroit who were anxious to earn $5 a day. Soon, trains coming into Detroit were filled with men looking for work. For African Americans living in the South, still treated as near slaves 50 years after the end of the Civil War, the news of high wages in Detroit spread like wildfire. Thousands began the trek north to the "Promised Land," where, it was said, wages were high and discrimination was nonexistent.

Writer LeRoi Jones wrote in his book *Blues People*, "Five-dollars a day was what Mr. Ford said, and Negroes came hundreds of miles to line up outside his employment offices."[11] Blues songs were written about working at the Ford Motor Company, where "a man is treated like a man."[12] Musician Blind Blake sang, "I'm goin' to Detroit, get myself a good job/ Tried to stay around here with the starvation mob/I'm goin' to get me a job in Mr. Ford's place, stop these eatless days from starin' me in the face."[13]

As Jones explained, "The name *Ford* became synonymous with northern opportunity, and the Ford Model T was one of the first automobiles Negroes could purchase—'the poor man's car.'"[14] Indeed, one of the many benefits to Ford of paying high wages was a simple one. His own workers could now afford to buy a Model T Ford of their very own.

MODEL T MANIA

With the invention of the automated assembly line, the car, which had long been considered a luxury item available to the rich, was now available to the majority of Americans. Not only was the Model T affordable, it was incredibly inexpensive to run and operate. While other cars cost as much as $1,500 a year to maintain, a Model T cost less than $100. (It was said that if the driver supplemented the standard Ford tool kit with a pipe wrench, a coil of bailing wire, a tire-patch kit, a spare inner tube, some bobby pins, and a pocket knife, that there was nothing he or she could not fix.)

It was the car that changed America, giving everyone the freedom to go anywhere they wanted, anytime they wanted to go. Farmers and others living in rural areas especially welcomed the freedom the car gave them to travel to see others. Farmers who had worked their horses hard all day could now use their car to visit friends in the evening, breaking the isolation so many suffered through. As the *Ford Times* boasted, "It has remodeled the social life of the country."[15]

And because the car was so simply built and so versatile, it was used for more than just transportation. By attaching a belt to the vehicle's crankshaft or rear axle, the farmer now had a limitless source of power available for virtually any task, including "grinding grain, sawing wood, filling silos, churning butter, shearing sheep, pumping water, elevating grain, shelling corn, turning grindstones, and washing clothes."[16] As one happy farmer's wife from Rome, Georgia, wrote to Henry Ford in 1918, "Your car lifted us out of the mud. It brought joy into our lives."[17]

Women, too, embraced the freedom that the Model T provided. It was considered to be one of the easiest gasoline-powered cars to operate, a fact that the Ford Motor Company was only too eager to publicize. "There is no complex shifting of gears to bother the driver. In fact there is very little machinery about the car—none that a woman cannot understand in a few minutes and learn to control with very little practice."[18]

Indeed, in its pamphlet titled "The Woman and the Ford," the company explicitly linked the freedom the car would bring women to the expanding freedoms that women were winning nationwide. "It has broadened her horizon—increased her pleasures—given new favor to her body—made neighbors of faraway friends—and multiplied tremendously her range of activity. It is a real weapon in the changing order. More than any other—the Ford's a woman's car."[19]

Everybody, it seemed, was driving a Model T Ford. Even famed aviator Charles Lindbergh, in his book *Boyhood on the Upper Mississippi*, had fond memories of his family's first car. It was a Model T Tourabout, equipped with the "standard foot-pedal gearshift, four cylinder engine, smooth-faced clincher-rim tires, carbide headlights, hand crank, squeeze rubber-bulb horn, folding waterproof cloth top, and quick fasten-onside curtains for rainy days."[20]

His mother named it "Maria," and, writing about the car in 1969, Lindbergh wrote rhapsodically about the changes it brought to his life. "Before Maria arrived, [automobiles] seemed almost as separate from our everyday lives as a show up on a stage. The fact that *my* father had bought an automobile was startling and amazing. It took my mother and me a long time to get accustomed to this new member of our family."[21]

Which is not to say, of course, that the transition from a horse-driven society to an automobile society always went smoothly. In his book, Lindbergh gives a lovely example of a confrontation between horse and car in the year 1912, when he was being given a ride into town on a local farmer's horse-drawn lumber wagon:

> Soon afterward an automobile approached and the horses began shying. The car stopped—a usual procedure for those days. The farmer asked me to hold the reins, jumped off the wagon, took the bridle of a horse in each hand, swung the team to the side of the road, and buried the horses' heads in

Ford's Model T was enormously popular with the American public, and women viewed the vehicle to be a symbol of modernity and freedom. The "Tin Lizzie" granted women more independence, as it allowed them to travel and experience the world outside of their homes and neighborhoods.

hazel bushes. The automobile ground by and the farmer led the horses back to the road and climbed onto the wagon. I handed him the reins. We jolted on silently for several minutes. Then he turned to me and said, "If they ever get them things so you can drive 'em with reins, I guess there'll be quite a lot of 'em."[22]

The Model T became a national obsession. Songs such as "The Little Ford Rambled Right Along" (1914) and "You Can't Afford to Marry, If You Can't Afford a Ford (1915)" were composed in its honor. Nobel Prize–winning author Sinclair Lewis wrote a novel, *Free Air*, about a cross-country trip he took in his Model T with his wife, Grace. Years later, Grace wrote in her memoir that the biggest thrill of her husband's life was the day he was able to pull up in front of the family house in his new Model T and ask, "How about a little ride?"[23]

As early as 1915, the car and its reputation had become so well known that a joke book, *The Original Ford Joke Book*, was published. The jokes, while corny by today's standards, illustrate the bemused attitude that even Model T drivers had toward their beloved car, as these examples suggest:

> One man invited another to ride with him in an old Ford. He got in. The man cranked up his machine. It began to jiggle up and down. "Does it always go like this?" asked the man who was invited for the ride.
> "No," replied the owner, "only when it's running."

> A RIDDLE
> What is the best family car?
> The Ford of course. It has a hood for mother, a muffler for father, and a rattle for the baby.

> A Ford owner had no speedometer. "I don't need one at all. At ten miles an hour the hood rattles, at fifteen the radiator rattles, at twenty the top rattles, and at twenty-five miles an hour the whole thing rattles."[24]

And it was more than just an American phenomenon. Douglas Brinkley pointed out that with the possible exception of the Singer sewing machine, no U.S.-made mechanical device was sold in so many places around the world. In 1910, even before the automated assembly line had dramatically increased its production, the *Ford Times* announced that the Model T was the first car to be sold in Kuala Lumpur, Turkey, Barbados, and Mauritius. The article went on to describe the worldwide reaction:

Naked little urchins on the narrow streets of Bombay dodge the rapidly moving cars. Scantily clothed Ethiopian giants pilot tourist-laden Ford cars through the mining districts of South Africa. The Sphinx, if he [sic] were to speak, would comment on the horseless steed of vanadium steel that so frequently is seen before it. . . . The narrow Jinrikisha roads of the new Japan are being rebuilt so that the pleasures of the American automobile may be enjoyed.[25]

When Pancho Villa, the Mexican revolutionary, was chased across the border back into Mexico by American troops, he used a Model T to escape into the mountains of northern Mexico. Missionary Marie Nelson mounted a loudspeaker to the hood of her Model T to allow her to preach to large crowds in Angola. In China, a newspaper editor commented that in his country, the words *automobile* and *Model T* had become synonymous.

This revolution in transportation, this worldwide phenomenon that changed people's lives in ways that are still being felt today, was largely due to Henry Ford and the automated assembly line. By discovering a way to manufacture products faster and on a greater scale than ever before, Ford was able to lower the price of something that, once a rarity, became an everyday item.

The automated assembly line had, indeed, caused a dramatic change not only in the way that products were manufactured, but in the relationship between manager and worker. In addition, it allowed the concept of mass production to become commonplace. By 1918, it was said by many that Henry Ford had become the world's first self-made billionaire, based solely on the success of the Model T he had built. But times were changing, customers' needs were changing, and the world that Henry Ford built at Highland Park would change as well.

Robots
on the Line

The Model T was so successful that by 1918 plans were put into action to build a new factory, the River Rouge Plant, in Dearborn, Michigan. It would be a masterpiece of industrial know-how.

With 53,000 machines being operated by 75,000 workers along 30 miles (48 km) of conveyer belts, it was the largest assembly line in the world. By 1928, to take a car from raw materials to completion took only four days. As demand increased for automobiles, more and more cars had to come off those 30 miles of assembly lines. The lines were sped up, making it more and more difficult for the workers to keep up.

Ford's $5 a day was no longer enough to keep workers happy. The call for unionization began in earnest, as workers banded together to speak with one voice. They wanted a system in which workers and management *both* had control over line speed.

Henry Ford, on the other hand, was strongly against unions. He felt that they did the workers more harm than good and that good managers could work to create a system in which unions were not necessary. Workers felt differently about this, and they insisted that their voices and demands be heard.

The struggle of workers to achieve their goals was a long and bloody one. In fact, it was not until June 1941 that Henry Ford, faced by his wife's threats to leave him if he did not give in, signed a contract with the automobile workers' union, the UAW. The days of profit sharing and strict control of the assembly lines and workers by management were now over.

Ford had other problems as well. Other automakers, such as General Motors (GM) and in particular its Chevrolet divi-

FORD AND THE WORLD WAR II EFFORT

It has been said that there is no demand like the demand caused by warfare. During war, a lot of things need to be made and lots of things are destroyed, which causes a huge demand for those products. So when the United States entered World War II in December 1941, one of its strongest assets was its assembly line–driven factories, of which none were larger or more important than those used by the automobile industry in Detroit, Michigan.

Production of civilian automobiles stopped for the duration of the war. Instead of cars, America's automobile factories, including Henry Ford's specially designed Willow Run plant, went to work manufacturing the tanks, jeeps, and airplanes needed to win the war. Willow Run, for example, which at 3.5 million square feet (325,161 sq. meters) was the largest assembly in the world at the time, was, at its peak of production, producing nearly 14 completed B-24 bombers *per day*.

sion, began making serious gains against Ford and his Model T. How did they do it? By approaching the manufacturing process and the needs of the consumer in an entirely new way.

A decision was reached at GM that the company would never be able to compete against Ford by producing a car for the masses of its own. Instead, it would focus on selling cars whose outward appearance would change annually, inspiring buyers to trade in their old cars for new ones each and every year. Historian Daniel Boorstin called this need the "search for novelty."[1]

Boorstin went on to describe the reasoning behind this new policy. "Americans would climb the ladder of consumption by abandoning the new for the newer."[2] Instead of selling cars based on utility and ease of use, automakers would begin to

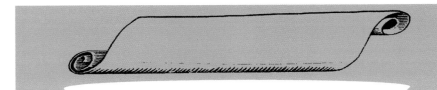

The assembly lines rolled nonstop, 24 hours a day. Pilots often slept on cots at the factory while they waited for their plane to come off the line. Women and African Americans, both of whom had previously been thought incapable of working on the line, were out of necessity brought in to work the lines to help America's war effort.

By the end of the war, nearly 90,000 bombers, 57,000 aircraft engines, and 250,000 tanks and jeeps had come off the Detroit assembly lines. Thanks to Henry Ford and his role in the development of the assembly line, America had the means necessary to win the war, because it could manufacture products faster and cheaper than anywhere else in the world. Indeed, thanks to Henry Ford, American factories could build jeeps, tanks, and aircraft faster than the Germans and the Japanese could destroy them.

Other manufacturers, including his competitors, adapted Ford's techniques to be faster and more cost-efficient. Forced to retire his beloved Model T, Ford had to reconfigure all of his factories, spending $250 million to refit his River Rouge factory (above), before he could build the new Model A.

sell cars based on style and comfort. The assembly line began to change as well, as manufactures began the move from single-purpose machines to standard machines that could be used to build parts for a variety of different models.

Car buyers began to purchase GM cars in greater and greater numbers, eager to trade in their old "Tin Lizzies" for newer, more luxurious styles of cars. Ford's market share plummeted, from 51 percent in 1921 down to just 30 percent in 1926. Faced with even worse numbers in 1927, Ford announced the end of the Model T. With 15 million Model Ts produced, the market was ready for Ford to move on and build a new kind of car.

It was, however, easier said than done. The Ford Motor Company's factory had been designed around the idea of building just one kind of car—the Model T. Ford was forced to completely retool its factories, because what worked for the Model T did not work for the new car, dubbed the Model A. The changeover proved difficult, not only because 5,580 new parts had to be designed and built, but because, as Ford's tool department chief William Pioch explained: "Mr. Ford's idea of a manufacturing plant was to get the machines as close together as possible to save floor space. It was a good idea, but it didn't work out too good [for changeovers] . . . because the machines were in so tight that sometimes if we had to move a machine, we'd have to move four or five different machines to get that one out."[3] It took nearly $250 million to reconfigure the River Rouge factory to build the Model A.

With that, an era was ended. The automated assembly line, created by Ford to build just one product, had grown to become more flexible. It was now designed to be redesigned quickly to meet the demands of a consumer society that expected the newest and best at all times. Products of all kinds were now rolling off the assembly line at ever faster speeds. Manufacturers producing all kinds of products were now using the assembly line and making it their own.

But no innovation remains static. Change is inevitable, and with the end of World War II in 1945, new ways to use the line, along with a new relationship between workers and management, began to take place. Ironically, that change took place in Japan—one of the nations that the United States defeated during the war.

POSTWAR CHANGES

At the end of World War II, Japan's industrial base, like the rest of the country, was in ruins. While this may seem to have presented the nation with a challenge, it was an opportunity as well. Forced to rebuild, Japanese companies such as Toyota had the freedom to start from scratch, to rethink both the assembly line and the way that workers were employed on the line.

In 1950, 1,000 vehicles a month were being built by the Toyota Motor Company. At the same time, 1,000 vehicles a day were being built by the Ford Motor Company. To compete, Toyota, which was the manufacturer of nearly all of Japan's trucks, automobiles, fire engines—everything—had to develop a new system of manufacture. Japan, though, was nearly broke and lacked natural resources. But what it did have in abundance was people.

So, instead of building assembly lines around machines, Toyota built its assembly lines around people—the idea being that people are more flexible than machines. Unlike American automobile companies, Toyota decided to use the workers' mind power and experience to build a new system from the ground up.

Work was reorganized to reduce waste of both materials and time. It was left up to the workers to define their responsibilities, in a process called "remanufacturing." Every job on the Toyota assembly line was defined and redefined by the worker doing that job. So with every step, the worker doing that job became more efficient.

Workers were also more fulfilled because they had a sense of pride and responsibility in their work. It was the workers themselves who were in charge of the quality, with the ability to stop the line at any time if they felt the quality of work was not there. Productivity increased, with more and more parts being manufactured in less and less time.

New techniques were developed. One of these was a radical improvement in die changing: The die is a hard piece of metal in the exact shape that sheet metals assume after pounding. Toyota's workers developed a system on rollers that allowed die changing to take place in 2 to 3 hours, versus 2 to 3 weeks in the United States. Forced to find ways to become flexible, the company found further ways to save time and money as well.

Instead of forcing their workers to become parts of a machine, Toyota created a team of skilled, motivated, and innovative workers responsible to the company to improve production methods. In a system known as "Kaizan," management would, for a given line, remove 10 percent of the workers, materials, resources, and time available to manufacture a given product.

It would then be up to the workers themselves to figure out how to get the job done. When that was accomplished, the process would be repeated, and then repeated again, until the company had found, through the workers' own initiative, the best and most efficient way to manufacture their product. So by the 1970s, Japanese automakers were ready to take advantage of their system to build the smaller, more fuel-efficient cars that were becoming more and more popular in the United States.

American automakers were still manufacturing cars as they had since the early days of Henry Ford: emphasizing quantity over quality; producing large, gas-guzzling cars; pushing workers to extremes; and using unskilled workers to do their jobs with absolutely no thinking required. The system that had worked so well for Henry Ford had been pushed to its limits—and was on the verge of a breakdown.

By 1980, Japan surpassed the United States in total automobile production. By 1989, the Japanese were making cars in half the time and with half the defects as in the United States. Finally, U.S. automakers began to see the light. The automated assembly line began, once again, to change and adapt to new challenges.

THE ASSEMBLY LINE TODAY

Today, the automated assembly line is more automated than ever before, with machines now doing more work. Jobs that were once done solely by people—welding and painting, for example—are now done by machines. In the case of welding, by using computer-based techniques, the job can be done more precisely than ever. In the case of painting, it is a health issue. Workers spraying large amounts of paint for eight hours a day are at risk for lung problems, so the job is one best left to machines.

In fact, during the last several decades, 37 percent of all assembly line jobs have been lost. This is because most workers on the assembly line are not doing actual work—they are there to monitor the robots that are doing the work. Many American manufacturers have finally learned what the Japanese have known for decades: humans are more flexible than machines. And, by figuring out which jobs are best done by machines and which are best done by people, there are now fewer people assembling more products.

Not only are robots doing more and more of the work once done by humans, but the virtual assembly line has changed the very way that manufacturing is done. Take, for example, an enormous product such as Boeing's 777 jet plane. Instead of having to work out the manufacturing process in the factory, the plane can be preassembled by virtual workers, using virtual parts, on a virtual assembly line.

By using this system, known as ebuild, engineers can see how the process works, make certain that every part fits, and most importantly, fix any problems before production has begun. (Imagine how much simpler Henry Ford's life would have been if he had been able to do this while switching production over from the Model T to the Model A.) With a 40 percent savings of time and money in the development of products, ebuilding reduces the time it takes to bring the "real" assembly line online.

But these changes, while they have improved the quality of the automobiles coming off the assembly line, have proved devastating to the employees who for generations had worked on those lines. Unemployment in Detroit today stands

Modern automobile factories, like this General Motors plant in Doraville, Georgia, have automated assembly lines. Computers and machines have become more precise, more efficient, and less costly than human workers, resulting in cheaper cars but also an increase in unemployment.

at 11.8 percent. According to U.S. census data, the city, once the fourth-largest in the nation with a peak population of 1,849,568, has fallen to number 19, with a population of just 713,777, lower than at any time since 1901. (Of course, there are other factors involved in Detroit's decline, including racial tension, white flight into the suburbs, crime, and drug abuse, but change in the automobile industry has played a major role in that decline.)

As we have seen, the assembly line, whose earliest origins can be traced back to the Chinese and the Assyrians, has played a major role in the development of the United States we know today. As the times have changed, the assembly line has changed with them. Henry Ford, whose first assembly line had automobile bodies built on the second floor go down a slide to the chassis below on the first floor, would be amazed to observe that less than 100 years later, jumbo jets are being designed and built on virtual assembly lines.

He would, however, recognize in those virtual assembly lines a link to those of his own. Both lines reflect humankind's ongoing drive to find more effective and time-saving ways to produce the products that consumers want to buy. From the terra-cotta warriors to muskets built at the Springfield Armory to the Singer Sewing Machine Company to Pope Bicycles to the Ford Motor Company and beyond, we have seen how one simple idea has grown and developed.

And as we look at that seemingly simple idea, we can see how it has changed the world in which we live. From clothing to computers, from furniture to packaged food, even to the very book that you're reading right now, items that once had to be made by hand are instead assembled, using interchangeable parts, on moving assembly lines. And because of that, just as Ford did with the Model T, manufacturers are able to produce these articles on an unimaginable scale, thereby lowering prices and making these items affordable for nearly everyone.

The consumer world in which we live, bombarded with advertisements for items to buy, items the ads tell us we need in order to be popular, to be fashionable, or just to keep up with the neighbors next door, can be directly traced to the changes brought about by Henry Ford and the automated assembly line. It will be fascinating to see the changes that take place on the assembly line in the years to come.

CHRONOLOGY

900–612 B.C.	Ancient Assyrians use bucket elevators called the "chain of pots" to speed up their manufacturing system.
215 B.C.	Emperor Shih Huang Ti orders terra-cotta army to be built. The parts are built at different workshops, to be assembled later at a central site.
A.D. 1300s	The Venetian Arsenal uses thousands of workers and prefabricated parts to produce one warship per day.
1765	French general Jean-Baptiste de Gribeauval begins a quest to build army weapons to one standard system, allowing parts of weapons to be easily interchanged. The system becomes known as *le système Gribeauval*.
1785	America's ambassador to France, Thomas Jefferson, sends a letter to John Jay explaining the system of interchangeability.
1798	Eli Whitney is given a contract to build 12,000 muskets for the U.S. Army.
By 1832	Gun manufacturers Simeon North and John Hall are able to mass-produce complex machines—guns—using a system close to interchangeability.
1853	The British Select Committee on Small Arms sends John Anderson to the United States to visit the Springfield Armory to study advances made in interchangeability and gun manufacture.
1863	**July 30** Henry Ford is born on a farm in Dearborn, Michigan.
1872	The Wheeler and Wilson Manufacturing Company builds 174,088 sewing machines, proving that larger, more complex items can be built using the armory system.

1873   The Singer Sewing Machine Company converts to the American system of manufactures, selling nearly 250,000 sewing machines.

1876   Nikolaus August Otto invents the four-stroke motor.

1885   Karl Benz builds his first automobile.

1887   The "safety" bicycle is introduced, starting a fad that leads to new advances in technology and manufacture, as well as the desire to build individual motorized vehicles.

1893   Charles and Frank Duryea found the Duryea Motor Company, becoming the first American automobile manufacturing company.

TIMELINE

900–612 B.C.
Ancient Assyrians use bucket elevators called the "chain of pots" to speed up their manufacturing system

1798
Eli Whitney is given a contract to build 12,000 muskets for the U.S. Army

1873
The Singer Sewing Machine Company converts almost entirely to the American system of manufactures, selling nearly 250,000 sewing machines

900 B.C. ———————————————————— **1896**

1765
French general Jean-Baptiste de Gribeauval begins a quest to build army weapons to one standard system, allowing parts of weapons to be easily interchanged

1863
July 30 Henry Ford is born on a farm in Dearborn, Michigan

1896
June 4 Henry Ford test-drives his first automobile, the Quadricycle, down the streets of Detroit

1893   Henry Ford builds his first gasoline engine.

1896   **June 4** Henry Ford test-drives his first automobile, the Quadricycle, down the streets of Detroit.

1899   Henry Ford founds the Detroit Automobile Company. It fails months later.

1901   Backed by a group of investors, Henry Ford founds the Henry Ford Company. Hired as the company's chief engineer, he has disagreements with management and leaves the company in 1902. The company later becomes the Cadillac Automobile Company.

1902   Ransom Eli Olds uses a primitive version of the assembly line to build 2,500 cars.

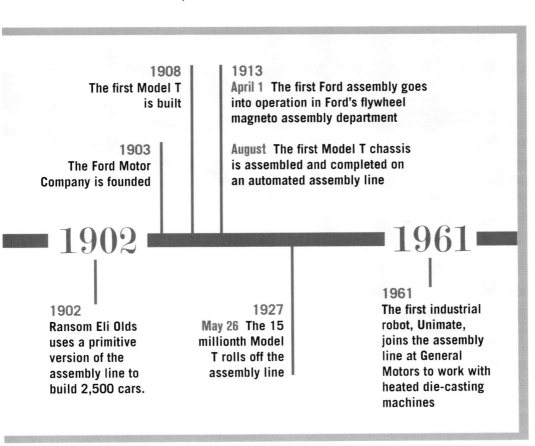

1908
The first Model T
is built

1913
April 1 The first Ford assembly goes into operation in Ford's flywheel magneto assembly department

1903
The Ford Motor
Company is founded

August The first Model T chassis is assembled and completed on an automated assembly line

1902   1961

1902
Ransom Eli Olds
uses a primitive
version of the
assembly line to
build 2,500 cars.

1927
May 26 The 15
millionth Model
T rolls off the
assembly line

1961
The first industrial
robot, Unimate,
joins the assembly
line at General
Motors to work with
heated die-casting
machines

1903   The Ford Motor Company is founded. Early model Fords such as the Models A and B do well but are not the inexpensive cars Ford hopes to build for the average worker.

1907   After a power struggle, Henry Ford becomes president of the Ford Motor Company, which allows him to build the car of his dreams.

1908   The first Model T is built, still using the conventional methods of the day. Work continues on Ford's new Highland Park plant, which will be devoted solely to the manufacture of Model Ts.

1913   **April 1** The first Ford assembly goes into operation in Ford's flywheel magneto assembly department.

   August The first Model T chassis is assembled and completed on an automated assembly line.

1927   **May 26** The 15 millionth Model T rolls off the assembly line.

1954   **March 25** The first color television rolls of the assembly line at Bloomington, Indiana.

1961   The first industrial robot, Unimate, joins the assembly line at General Motors to work with heated die-casting machines.

Notes

CHAPTER ONE

1. *Modern Marvels: Assembly Line*, DVD, The History Channel, 2009.
2. David A. Hounshell, *From the American System to Mass Production: 1800–1932*. Baltimore, Md.: Johns Hopkins University Press, 1985, p. 316.
3. Ben Hamper, *Rivethead: Tales from the Assembly Line*. New York: Warner Books, 1991, p. 2.
4. Douglas Brinkley, *Wheels for the World: Henry Ford, His Company, and a Century of Progress, 1903–2003*. New York: Penguin Books, 2004, p. 152.

CHAPTER TWO

1. Hounshell, *From the American System to Mass Production*, p. 26.
2. Hounshell, *From the American System to Mass Production*, p. 31.
3. Ibid.
4. Diana Muir, *Reflections in Bullough's Pond: Economy and Ecosystem in New England*. Hanover, N.H.: UPNE, 2002, p. 276.
5. Hounshell, *From the American System to Mass Production*, p. 61.
6. Hounshell, *From the American System to Mass Production*, p. 64.
7. Hounshell, *From the American System to Mass Production*, p. 62.

CHAPTER THREE

1. Hounshell, *From the American System to Mass Production*, p. 67.
2. Hounshell, *From the American System to Mass Production*, p. 69.

3. Hounshell, *From the American System to Mass Production*, p. 84.
4. Hounshell, *From the American System to Mass Production*, p. 85.
5. Hounshell, *From the American System to Mass Production*, p. 109.

CHAPTER FOUR

1. Hounshell, *From the American System to Mass Production*, p. 189.
2. Hounshell, *From the American System to Mass Production*, p. 190.
3. Hounshell, *From the American System to Mass Production*, p. 214.
4. Ibid.
5. Ibid.
6. Ibid.

CHAPTER SIX

1. Henry Ford, with Samuel Crowther, *My Life and Work*. Public domain books, 2008, Kindle edition, locations 257–269.
2. Brinkley, *Wheels for the World*, p. 7.
3. Ibid.
4. Ibid.
5. Ibid.
6. Brinkley, *Wheels for the World*, p. 8.
7. Brinkley, *Wheels for the World*, p. 11.
8. Ibid.
9. John Bankston, *Henry Ford and the Assembly Line*. Bear, Del.: Mitchell Lane Publishers, 2004, p. 19.
10. Bankston, *Henry Ford and the Assembly Line*, p. 30.

11. Brinkley, *Wheels for the World*, p. 22.
12. Bankston, *Henry Ford and the Assembly Line*, p. 33.

CHAPTER SEVEN

1. Brinkley, *Wheels for the World*, p. 70.
2. Hounshell, *From the American System to Mass Production*, p. 218.
3. "Henry Ford Changes the World, 1908." EyeWitness to History, 2005. http://www.eyewitnessto history.com/ford.htm.
4. Ibid.
5. Hounshell, *From the American System to Mass Production*, p. 218.
6. "Quote." PlanetThoughts. http://www.planetthoughts. org/?pg=pt/Whole&qid=2253.
7. Hounshell, *From the American System to Mass Production*, p. 221.
8. Hounshell, *From the American System to Mass Production*, p. 247.
9. David E. Nye, *Consuming Power: A Social History of American Energies*. Cambridge, Mass.: MIT Press, 2001, p. 143.
10. Brinkley, *Wheels for the World*, p. 155.
11. Brinkley, *Wheels for the World*, pp. 180–181.

CHAPTER EIGHT

1. *Modern Marvels: Assembly Line.*
2. Brinkley, *Wheels for the World*, p. 159.
3. Ibid.
4. Brinkley, *Wheels for the World*, p. 161.
5. Ibid.
6. Brinkley, *Wheels for the World*, p. 162.

7. Ibid.
8. Brinkley, *Wheels for the World*, p. 163.
9. Brinkley, *Wheels for the World*, p. 169.
10. Brinkley, *Wheels for the World*, p. 170.
11. Brinkley, *Wheels for the World*, p. 171.
12. Ibid.
13. Ibid.
14. Ibid.
15. Brinkley, *Wheels for the World*, p. 128.
16. Ibid.
17. Ibid.
18. Brinkley, *Wheels for the World*, p. 118.
19. Ibid.
20. Charles Lindbergh, *Boyhood on the Upper Mississippi: A Reminiscent Letter*. St. Paul: Minnesota Historical Society, 1971, p. 25.
21. Ibid.
22. Lindbergh, *Boyhood on the Upper Mississippi*, p. 27.
23. Brinkley, *Wheels for the World*, p. 122.
24. *The Original Ford Joke Book.* Binghamton, N.Y.: Woodward Publishing Company, 1915. http://www.vintageantiqueclassics.com/ford-joke-book.html.
25. Brinkley, *Wheels for the World*, p. 131.

CHAPTER NINE

1. Hounshell, *From the American System to Mass Production*, p. 263.
2. Hounshell, *From the American System to Mass Production*, p. 264.
3. Hounshell, *From the American System to Mass Production*, p. 287.

BIBLIOGRAPHY

"Assembly Line—History," Science Encyclopedia. Available online. URL: http://science.jrank.org/pages/558/Assembly-Line-History.html.

Bankston, John. *Henry Ford and the Assembly Line*. Bear, Del.: Mitchell Lane Publishers, 2004.

Bellis, Mary. "The Duryea Brothers—Automobile History," About.com. Available online. URL: http//inventors.about.com/od/dstartinventors/a/DuryeaBrothers.htm?p=1.

Brinkley, Douglas. *Wheels for the World: Henry Ford, His Company, and a Century of Progress, 1903-2003*. New York: Penguin Books, 2004.

Ford, Henry, with Samuel Crowther. *My Life and Work*. Public domain books, Kindle edition, 2008.

Hamper, Ben. *Rivethead: Tales from the Assembly Line*. New York: Warner Books, 1991.

"Henry Ford Changes the World, 1908," EyeWitness to History, 2005. Available online. URL: http://www.eyewitnesstohistory.com/ford.htm.

Henry Ford Museum. Available online. URL: http://www.hfmgv.org/museum/index.aspx.

"The History of the Automobile," About.com. Available online. http://inventors.about.com/library/weekly/aacarsgasa.htm?p=1.

Hounshell, David A. *From the American System to Mass Production: 1800–1932*. Baltimore, Md.: Johns Hopkins University Press, 1985.

Lindbergh, Charles A. *Boyhood on the Upper Mississippi: A Reminiscent Letter.* St. Paul: Minnesota Historical Society, 1972.

Modern Marvels: Assembly Line. DVD. The History Channel, 2009.

Muir, Diana. *Reflections in Bullough's Pond: Economy and Ecosystem in New England.* Hanover, N.H.: UPNE, 2002.

Nye, David E. *Consuming Power: A Social History of American Energies.* Cambridge, Mass.: MIT Press, 2001.

The Original Ford Joke Book. Binghamton, N.Y.: Woodward Publishing Company, 1915. Available online. http://www .vintageantiqueclassics.com/ford-joke-book.html.

Petty, Ross D. "Peddling the Bicycle in the 1890s: Mass Marketing Shifts into High Gear." *Journal of Macromarketing,* 1995. Available online. http://jmk.sagepub.com/cgi/content/ abstract/15/1/32.

"Quote," PlanetThoughts. Available online. http://www.planet thoughts.org/?pg=pt/Whole&qid=2253.

Sweezy, Paul M. "Cars and Cities." *Monthly Review,* vol. 51, no. 11. Available online. http://www.monthlyreview.org/400 pms.htm.

Further Reading

Collins, Tom. *The Legendary Model-T Ford: The Ultimate History of America's First Great Automobile.* Iola, Wis.: Krause Publications, 2007.

De Santis, Solange. *Life on the Line: One Woman's Tale of Work, Sweat, and Survival.* New York: Anchor Books, 2000.

Herlihy, David B. *Bicycle: The History.* New Haven, Conn.: Yale University Press, 2006.

Kimes, Beverly R. *Pioneers, Engineers, and Scoundrels: The Dawn of the Automobile in America.* Warrendale, Pa.: SAE International, 2004.

Olsen, Barney, and Joseph Cabadas. *The American Auto Factory* (Automotive History and Personalities). St. Paul, Minn.: MBI Publishing Company, 2002.

Tarkington, Booth. *The Magnificent Ambersons.* Scotts Valley, Calif.: CreateSpace, 2009.

White, E.B. *Farewell to Model T and From Sea to Shining Sea.* New York: Little Bookroom, 2003.

PHOTO CREDITS

INDEX

ABOUT THE AUTHOR

DENNIS ABRAMS is the author of numerous books for Chelsea House, including biographies of Barbara Park, Xerxes, Albert Pujols, Rachael Ray, Nicolas Sarkozy, and Jay-Z, and the history title *The Treaty of Nanjing*. He attended Antioch College, where he majored in English and communications. A voracious reader since the age of three, Dennis lives in Houston, Texas, with his partner of 20 years, along with their two cats and their dog, Junie B.